"This thought-provoking, challenging and often heart-rending book had a profound impact on me. I heartily recommend it to all followers of Christ who want to be challenged to take their faith more seriously."
Christine Sine, executive director, Mustard Seed Associates

"This is one of just a handful of books since Tolstoy to take Christ's Sermon on the Mount seriously, suggesting Jesus intended us to live his message rather than finding loopholes around it."
Brad Jersak, author of *Can You Hear Me? Tuning In to the God Who Speaks*

"*The Cost of Community* chronicles the joys and heartaches of living Jesus' blueprint for holiness—and provides us with the challenge and courage to 'do likewise.'"
Albert Haase, O.F.M., author of *Living the Lord's Prayer*

"In each generation there are those who carry on the spirit of Francis of Assisi. God knows that the church needs them! Jamie Arpin-Ricci is one of these, right here and right now, in his life and in this important book."
Jon M. Sweeney, author of *The St. Francis Prayer Book*

"A fresh and challenging exposition of the Sermon on the Mount, illustrated both from the life of Francis of Assisi and the contemporary experience of an inner-city community in Winnipeg, rooted in the strange but persuasive conviction that Jesus' teaching is to be obeyed rather than admired."
Stuart Murray Williams, Anabaptist Network, United Kingdom

"Jamie Arpin-Ricci holds our feet to the fire with the humility of one who himself continues to wrestle with the implications of taking Jesus at his word."
Sean Gladding, author of *The Story of God, the Story of Us*

"The familiar terrain of the Sermon on the Mount yields fresh insights and challenges in this grace-filled book."
Christine D. Pohl, Ph.D., professor of social ethics, Asbury Theological Seminary

"This book deserves two thumbs up from any who read it."
Tony Campolo, Eastern University

"Jamie Arpin-Ricci aptly exposes the spiritual laziness of Western Christianity and invites us to examine the way we live our faith. You will be simultaneously challenged and encouraged—encouraged that as you give your life away, you will receive a life more abundant and fulfilling than you can imagine."
Phileena Heuertz, international director, Word Made Flesh, and author of *Pilgrimage of a Soul*

"If you read this book carefully, and reflect on how Jamie and his faith community are following Jesus, you will soon realize that while the cost of discipleship is great, the cost of nondiscipleship is even greater."
JR Woodward, cofounder of Kairos LA and the Ecclesia Network

"Jamie Arpin-Ricci lives and writes authentically in conversation with his community, the hard neighborhood he lives in, a thirteenth-century saint and Jesus. I love his humble honesty as he wrestles in that all-important place where ideals and reality meet."
Kent Annan, author of *After Shock* and *Following Jesus Through the Eye of the Needle*

"*The Cost of Community* reminds me that following Jesus is both a dangerous and demanding undertaking if we honestly embrace his invitation 'to hear my words and do likewise.'"
Richard Twiss, Sicangu Lakota, president, Wiconi International

"This gentle memoir makes both the Sermon on the Mount and St. Francis real for us today."
Scot McKnight, author, *One.Life: Jesus Calls, We Follow* and *The King Jesus Gospel*

"Jamie Arpin-Ricci has succeeded in producing a volume that is both fresh and challenging. It has helped me—and I hope it helps many others—to understand anew what it means not only to hear the words of Jesus but to put them into practice."
Dewi Hughes, theological advisor, Tearfund, and author of *Power and Poverty*

THE COST OF COMMUNITY

Jesus, St. Francis and Life in the Kingdom

JAMIE ARPIN-RICCI, C.J.

Foreword by **Jonathan Wilson-Hartgrove**

An imprint of InterVarsity Press
Downers Grove, Illinois

InterVarsity Press
P.O. Box 1400, Downers Grove, IL 60515-1426
World Wide Web: www.ivpress.com
E-mail: email@ivpress.com

InterVarsity Press® is the book-publishing division of InterVarsity Christian Fellowship/USA®, a movement of students and faculty active on campus at hundreds of universities, colleges and schools of nursing in the United States of America, and a member movement of the International Fellowship of Evangelical Students. For information about local and regional activities, write Public Relations Dept., InterVarsity Christian Fellowship/USA, 6400 Schroeder Rd., P.O. Box 7895, Madison, WI 53707-7895, or visit the IVCF website at <www.intervarsity.org>.

All Scripture quotations, unless otherwise indicated, are taken from the Holy Bible, New International Version®. NIV®. Copyright ©1973, 1978, 1984 by International Bible Society. Used by permission of Zondervan Publishing House. All rights reserved.

While all stories in this book are true, some names and identifying information in this book have been changed to protect the privacy of the individuals involved.

Cover design: Cindy Kiple
Interior design: Beth Hagenberg
Images: inner-city decay: slobo/iStockphoto
  St. Francis of Assisi: St. Francis of Assisi at Museo Francescano. Alinari/Regione Umbria/ Art Resource, NY

ISBN 978-0-8308-3635-2

Printed in the United States of America ∞

Library of Congress Cataloging-in-Publication Data

Arpin-Ricci, Jamie, 1977-
  The cost of community: Jesus, Francis, and life in the kingdom /
Jamie Arpin-Ricci.
    p. cm.
  Includes bibliographical references (p.   ).
  ISBN 978-0-8308-3635-2 (pbk.: alk. paper)
  1. Sermon on the mount—Criticism, interpretation, etc. 2.
Christian life. 3. Jesus Christ—Words. 4. Francis, of Assisi,
Saint, 1182-1226. 5. Arpin-Ricci, Jamie, 1977- I. Title.
  BT380.3.A77 2011
  226.9'06—dc23

                                                                            2011023112

| P | 18 | 17 | 16 | 15 | 14 | 13 | 12 | 11 | 10 | 9 | 8 | 7 | 6 | 5 | 4 | 3 | 2 | 1 |
| Y | 26 | 25 | 24 | 23 | 22 | 21 | 20 | 19 | 18 | 17 | 16 | 15 | 14 | 13 | 12 | 11 |

To my precious son,

Micah James Nigatu Arpin-Ricci.

When I look at your smile, I cannot help but declare:

"Who is like God?"

Contents

Foreword

In Canada, the day after Christmas is Boxing Day. I've read that it's the largest retail spending day of the year up there (akin to America's Black Friday, which follows our Thanksgiving feast). Inheritors of the largest economy to ever exist on earth, we North Americans celebrate our holidays on both sides of the border with great demonstrations of abundance—and we come down from our consumption by . . . shopping. If there is any single temptation that North Americans share, it's the persistent call of *One More Thing*.

But for Christians, the day after Christmas is a day to remember Stephen the Martyr. Our great celebration of Jesus coming to dwell among us is followed by a solemn reminder of what Jesus actually said about following him—that it leads to a cross in this world. Incarnation is good news not because it offers us a way out of the mess of this world, but because it shows us what God's love looks like here and now. Jesus' birth is followed by his death and resurrection, just as the birth of the church is followed by the witness of those who are willing to lay down their lives for the sake of the gospel. And so the good news spreads.

When we pay attention to the peculiar memory of the church, we hear the echoes of a quiet revolution—the gentle insistence that the way things are is not the way things have to be. Another world is possible; indeed, another world has already begun. We can be part of it now, but it costs nothing less than everything.

That Jesus took on human flesh and moved into the neighborhood means we have seen the way of love lived out. We know what
it looks like. In first-century Palestine, it meant that Jesus went to
Golgotha. It looked like Stephen praying for his enemies while they
threw the stones that would kill him. But what does it look like to
live God's love in our world today? What if you're not a wandering
preacher from Galilee, living under Roman occupation? What if
your greatest temptation is the alluring call of One More Thing on
the day after you've eaten ham and opened presents?

The church remembers saints because their witness is a reminder to us that we can follow Jesus from anywhere, anytime.
We don't forget the stories of the first believers. But neither do we
overlook the upper-class housewife who gave everything for the
kingdom or the soldier who met Jesus and left everything to follow him. Search the lives of the saints—read their stories closely—
and you will see in them your own story. They come from the
places we come from. And they show us what it means to follow
Jesus from here.

This is how Jamie Arpin-Ricci came to follow Jesus by following Francis of Asissi. Like Francis, Jamie has a father who's Italian
and a mother who's French. He grew up in a pious, respectable
home. He was born in the land of plenty. Jamie wanted to follow
the good way that Jesus outlines in his Sermon on the Mount, but
he wasn't sure how. What does it look like for a middle-class kid
to turn the other cheek, give to whoever asks and build his house
on the only foundation that will last? If Jesus gave him the road
map, the Holy Spirit gave Francis as his guide.

But this is not just a story about Jamie. It is a testimony to what
God has been doing in and through Little Flowers Community in
Winnipeg, Manitoba. A couple of years ago, I had occasion to visit
Winnipeg as a guest of local churches, come to share about a little
underground movement in the church called "new monasticism."

I described how young people in North America—people who've seen the lie in the gospel of One More Thing—have been coming together to establish communities of discipleship where they can experiment with what it looks like to follow Jesus twenty-four hours a day, seven days a week. In pulpits and lecture halls for four days straight I told my best stories, hoping to send a spark flying that might light a fire in Winnipeg. Over and again people asked me: do you know Little Flowers? An underground movement, yes. But it was already aflame.

Why do we need a story about a community in Winnipeg to help us hear the story of Francis so we can see more clearly what it means to live the story of Jesus? The answer is in these pages, but I'll give you a clue—it has something to do with the fact that God's best plan for saving the world is to put on flesh and live among us.

Jonathan Wilson-Hartgrove

Introduction

Despite the fact that I grew up in a good Christian home and as part of a solid church community, it was a bedraggled Italian beggar who first truly introduced me to the Sermon on the Mount and disrupted my life forever. To make matters more interesting, this odd son of a cloth merchant had been dead for nearly eight centuries! St. Francis of Assisi, beyond the stereotype of bird baths and hippy associations, is one of the most radical and impacting figures in the history of the church, in large part due to being faithful to one of his most deeply held convictions: *that Jesus actually meant us to do what he taught us, especially in the Sermon on the Mount.*

Few Christians would deny that Jesus wants us to live out his teachings in our lives, but through creative interpretation, consideration of context and many other means—some legitimate, others not—we have too often reduced what that kind of obedience actually requires of us. Not so with Francis. When Francis heard Jesus proclaim "Blessed are the poor," it could only mean one thing: that his wealth was holding him back from the blessings of God! And so, inspired by this absolutist conviction, Francis gave away everything he owned (to the point of literal nakedness) and followed Christ as a poor man, sharing life among those on the margins of society and the church. While we can fairly say that

Francis missed the more nuanced meaning of Jesus' words at times, it is hard to deny that, even in light of this somewhat uncritical literalism, he encountered and embodied Christ in such powerful ways that he was, indeed, quite blessed.

For all his idiosyncrasies and extremes, St. Francis of Assisi faithfully lived the words of Jesus. His commitment to God over *Mammon* meant that he refused to even touch money, forbidding his fellow friars from also doing so (Matthew 6:24). When he heard that God clothed the flowers with loving elegance and cared for the birds, he dedicated himself to treating creation with the love and respect of a brother (Matthew 6:26-29). And convinced that God would provide for all who asked, he and his brothers chose the life of mendicants, going door to door begging for the basic food and shelter they needed to live (Matthew 7:7). Again and again the teaching of the Sermon on the Mount inspired an unlikely and uncommon obedience in Francis, an obedience that defied logic and expectation when it went on to spark an ongoing reformation in the church even to this day.[1]

Of course, I was familiar with the Sermon on the Mount text of Matthew 5–7, but I had always heard individual verses or smaller sections read out of context. Whether it was the golden rule ("Do to others what you would have them do to you") or the Sunday school song "The Wise Man Built His House Upon the Rock," I had heard these sound bites as moral maxims, failing to see that by pulling them out of the broader context of Jesus' teaching their meaning changes significantly. The parable of the builders is particularly telling, for while it is commonly used to teach children the important lesson of "building your life on the Lord Jesus Christ" (as opposed to those who do not accept Jesus—the foolish ones), in context we see that it is the people of God who are at risk of being either foolish or wise. In fact, anyone who hears the words of the Sermon on the Mount and does not live them Jesus calls a fool. I had never heard such a connection made, obvious though it is in the text.

So I had never considered all three chapters as a unified teaching to be understood and applied together.[2] And yet as I studied the life of this thirteenth-century saint, I began to see how Jesus' words spoken on the hillside that day figured centrally into the commitments and lifestyle that shaped Francis and the broader Franciscan tradition. I began to wonder if others through Christian history had so intentionally embraced such a passion for this text. I knew that the Anabaptists (the tradition I have come to largely identify with) strongly embraced it, but I was surprised to learn that Francis was not alone in his commitment to live the words of Jesus found in the Sermon.

Leo Tolstoy, considered perhaps the greatest novelist of all time, centered his entire faith on the Sermon on the Mount, seeing Jesus' command to "turn the other cheek" (Matthew 5:38-42) as the cornerstone for his convictions about pacifism and nonviolence. Tolstoy's writing on the topic significantly influenced Mohandas Gandhi (who also came to deeply respect Jesus and his Sermon on the Mount) in the nature and direction of his own movement. In fact, Gandhi is said to have read the Sermon on the Mount twice a day for the last forty years of his life. Dietrich Bonhoeffer, a German Lutheran pastor and theologian, practiced the Sermon on the Mount to the point where he became an enemy of the Nazi state. He powerfully expressed his belief about the Sermon in his now classic book *The Cost of Discipleship.* Martin Luther King Jr., martyred pastor, activist and civil rights champion, also saw the Sermon on the Mount as the bedrock of his theology and philosophy for bringing nonviolent revolution and kingdom change to the world around him. These are just a few of those who changed our world as a result of Christ's word and example transforming their own lives. And it was not lost on me how many of these people paid for such devotion with their lives.

As I moved deeper into this study, I began to see the potential implications (and costs) for such a commitment in my own life and ministry. A few years earlier my wife, Kim, and I had moved into one of the inner-city communities of Winnipeg, Canada, to plant a new ministry with Youth With A Mission (YWAM). As we considered Jesus' radical commitment to enter meaningfully into our world as a human, we likewise felt called to enter fully into this new neighborhood. That meant changing our paradigm about what it means to "do ministry." No longer could we view the mission as "our job," commuting each day and putting in our hours. Instead, we realized that such a calling required complete immersion—incarnation as West End Winnipeggers.

Much to my mother's initial chagrin, we purchased an abandoned gang house—renovated by the aptly named ministry Lazarus Housing—and moved into the neighborhood, making it our home. Surrounded by poverty, substance abuse, violence and racism, we were daily confronted with the hard reality of being Christians in a context that was often less than welcoming. We were also confronted by our own shallow assumptions, "easy believisms" and half-measures. Several of our suspicions were immediately confirmed: many of the strategies and programs that worked well in more affluent communities did not work here. In many ways we were starting from scratch.

It was St. Francis's commitment to live in solidarity with the poor, as an expression of his allegiance to Christ, that first led me to him. And it was Francis's radically embodied (if sometimes extreme) commitment to live the words of Jesus in the Sermon on the Mount that opened my eyes to the possibility of a way of life and faith that we had never considered before, one that promised the richest blessings, but exacted the highest price. Were we willing to follow Francis in the footsteps of Jesus? Were we willing to defy convention and experiment with what it means to be obedient to Christ? Were we ready to pay the price to enter this costly kingdom of God?

It would be arrogant of me to compare our lives to Francis's, or even to compare to him those who have chosen to live among the poor in much more sacrificial ways than I have. However, this journey with Francis has only just begun, and the impact has already been humbling, wonderful and difficult. Francis's abandonment of his wealth has caused us to consider our own wealth, teaching us to intentionally embrace simplicity. Not only is this freeing us from the distractions of "stuff," but it's also liberating us from the fear and protectionism that all too often keep us from fully entering into relationship with the poor. When we opened our home to a schizophrenic homeless guy, we were made aware of the things that we value most. (I am ashamed to admit how long such fear held me back, and sometimes still does.)

The point is that Francis was too much like myself to ignore.[3] We both come from modest but relatively secure financial and stable social backgrounds. We both had promising careers in the family business. We both could have followed the pattern set out for us and it would have still been a good, even Christian, life. So Francis's choice of radical obedience to Christ led me to ask: *Why couldn't I be so unwaveringly devoted? What is holding me back from embracing the teachings and example of Christ so meaningfully?* When I realized that the differences were largely based on my own choices, I knew that God was calling me to something more. And slowly, step by step, I have begun to take that journey. I am just grateful that I do not have to make that trip alone.

LITTLE FLOWERS COMMUNITY

In all honesty, it has been a trying journey thus far—one we are still on—but we are slowly and at times clumsily beginning to let our lives and ministries be more intentionally shaped and guided by the Sermon on the Mount. Desiring to build genuine relationships with our neighbors and create a space for the development of a safe community, where it was often all too rare, we opened a small used bookstore, The Dusty Cover. While people initially came for the free fair-trade coffee and comfortable couches, relationships began to take root as people saw that, while unashamedly Christian, we were not using the store for any form of "bait and switch" evangelism. Soon a small core of people began to connect with each other through these times, leading to us visiting each other's homes and sharing a meal or two throughout the week.

Before long a regular weekly meal was happening with our new friends at the mission house where we lived with our fellow YWAM missionaries. We'd talk and laugh, play games and tell stories. As trust grew, we shared about life challenges, encouraged one another and even spent time praying together. Then, on just such an evening, a few of the regulars approached me with a sheepish grin. One of them spoke up and said, "Uh, Jamie, can we ask you something? I think we've become a church. Will you be our pastor?"

While we were thrilled at this development, we wanted to be sure this was God's plan for us, so we prayed about it. In the end we decided to accept the challenge and be more intentional about coming together as a community of faith and mission. After approaching a local Anabaptist denomination to partner with us, Little Flowers Community was born.[4] Gathering each week to share a potluck meal, we would spend time in prayer, worship and meditation on God's Word, with the explicit intention of trying to better understand what it means for us to obediently live the words of Jesus together. Inevitably this led to committed relationship with one another and to a community that surpassed formal church gatherings or programs. It meant welcoming people from our neighborhood into our community, faced with the challenges of poverty, mental illness, addiction and so much more. Soon we had a rather unique community of thirty or forty people, something of a church of misfit toys. It was difficult, and we made many mistakes along the way, but for many of us it was the truest experience of church and faith and mission we had ever experienced.

BROTHER ASS

Why did such a commitment to the Sermon on the Mount result in such a change? What made Jesus' teaching in this text stand out to us and draw us into this shared life of love and service? While we will explore this in more detail throughout the book, the most significant aspect of this teaching that stirred our imaginations and the burning conviction in our hearts was Jesus' emphasis to actually *do* what he taught us. Many of us who grew up in the church had primarily approached Jesus in a spirit of worship and humility. Now we were being inspired to also obey him. Do not misunderstand me. We were always taught to obey Jesus, but more often than not this commitment was reduced to important but ultimately inadequate emphases on being morally pure and religiously devoted. In other words, don't swear, drink or have sex before marriage, but rather go to church, read your Bible and witness to people about Jesus. Though these things are far from unimportant, many of us felt like there was something more, something we were missing.

I discovered the missing piece in the example of St. Francis. Born in the High Middle Ages, Francis was only passingly familiar with the details of the life and teachings of Christ, as were most Christians of his day. For centuries the church was an institution of power, shaping the lives of everyday people and nations alike. Being a Christian was assumed, which contributed to deep nominalism. A person did not choose to be a Christian; he or she was born one. In fact, individuals had to choose to not be a Christian, which was rare enough. As a result, many parts of the church had been corrupted by power-mongering, greed and nepotism. While many people were quite devoted, especially some of the commoners, a large segment just went through the motions, paying their tithes and rents to the church, participating in religious events only insofar as was beneficial or required. In other words, Francis was born into a time when Jesus was widely worshiped as God and placated as Savior, but rarely obeyed as Lord and Master. That kind of devotion was reserved for those with the special vocation to live cloistered lives of prayer and self-sacrifice—monks and nuns. Even priests were not expected to be especially devout.

Yet when Francis began to pursue the actual words of Jesus, he was naive enough to believe that Jesus meant what he said. While we cannot deny that he took his understanding to extremes from time to time, neither can we ignore the impact that such obedience had on Francis and on the world around him. He quickly became a living example of what it means to follow Jesus.[5] Through this radical devotion millions have been inspired to ask the same questions about their own faith. As the influence of the same Christendom that shaped Francis's time begins to come to an end in our own, the example of this *il poverello* (little poor man) has never been more important.

Few people in history have attempted to live out the teachings and example of Jesus more explicitly than St. Francis. As he did so, he found that the greatest hindrance to this devotion was himself. So mulish was his body to the cost of this obedience that he began to call his body "Brother Ass," bringing to mind the image of a stubborn donkey refusing to budge. He did not like to fast, to go without a blanket or to walk miles through the hills to proclaim the gospel. He balked at the unwavering demands of following Christ's teaching so very explicitly. Francis was well aware that beyond the appeal of Christian idealism was the hard reality of the cost of following Christ.

I think it is high time for the image of Brother (or Sister) Ass to experience something of a renaissance. After all, which of us cannot identify with that impossibly stubborn nature that rears its head whenever we are called to do something we do not want to do? Perhaps it is already making a comeback, such as with the logo for Likewise, a line of books that highlight the active faith of those who are doing what Francis did—obeying Christ in everyday life. While the name is an obvious reference to Jesus' challenge following the parable of the good Samaritan for his followers to "go and do likewise," the logo—the image of a man attempting to lead a clearly stubborn donkey with a rope—captures the reality that St. Francis saw so clearly. It is one thing to read and be inspired by the Sermon on the Mount, but what would it truly mean to go and do likewise and live the words of Jesus? While some would argue otherwise, I am convinced this is exactly what Jesus wants his followers to do on hearing his words. After all, in the closing parable of the Sermon, Jesus likens to fools those who hear his teaching but do not *do* what he says! He was also well aware that when the rubber (or hoof) hit the road, many of us wouldn't really want to pay such a price. So I was excited and honored to have our story counted among the Likewise titles; the idea (and logo) capture the heart of St. Francis.

If we are honest, all of us are guilty of looking for ways to minimize or avoid the true cost of discipleship. As G. K. Chesterton so poignantly stated, "The Christian ideal has not been tried and found wanting; it has been found difficult and left untried." Indeed, we should not be surprised that we do not want to follow this path, or even feel guilty for not wanting to. Even Jesus asked for the suffering he faced to be taken from him. For as Jesus made very clear, following him leads in one clear direction. "When Christ calls a man, he bids him come and die."[6] It is no sin for us to *wish* to avoid the cost of the cross, but it is sin when that desire makes us unwilling to follow him in obedience. It is a cross we must take up daily in sacrificial obedience to live as Christ commands—not as though such devotion saves us, but rather because it is the only authentic response to the unmerited gift of grace that we receive through Christ.

What emerges from such radical obedience is the very kingdom of God breaking into the broken reality of our lives, our neighborhoods and our world to shine as a living alternative of hope and salvation. It is a kingdom of peace, grace, forgiveness, hope, reconciliation and, above all, love. However, it is also a kingdom that was purchased at the ultimate price, a kingdom that demands we follow Christ to the cross, even daily, so that by his grace and the power of his Spirit, we can be reborn as his body, united to his purpose. Scot McKnight writes, "When Jesus was talking about the kingdom of God, he was thinking of concrete realities on earth, he was thinking of the Church being the embodiment of the Jesus dream, and he was thinking of you and I living together in community as we should."[7]

Setting the Stage

Matthew 4; 5:1-2

Like many young men of the medieval era, Francis of Assisi was enamored with the cult of chivalry, lapping up the stories of brave knights and great battles told by troubadours, traveling French singers and storytellers. Whether it was tales of King Arthur and the Knights of the Round Table or St. George slaying a dragon, he could not get enough of the romantic and noble tales. He soon became a masterful storyteller in his own right, earning the place of leader among his friends, an unlikely achievement for one not born to nobility. Above all, however, Francis dreamed of becoming a knight himself, riding out to battle to earn his place in songs and legends. And so it was that at the age of twenty Francis and many of his comrades rode off to war with the neighboring city of Perugia.

Francis's dreams of glory, however, would not come to fruition. Saved only because his wealthy father might pay a fair ransom for his son, the defeated young dreamer was thrown into a Perugian jail, staying there for an entire year. In the cold, filthy dungeon, Francis became ill with a sickness that followed him home after his release, leaving him weakened and prone to sickness for years to come. A few years later he attempted a second campaign as a wannabe knight. This time, however, his plans were foiled by something far more unexpected—a mysterious dream from God. While he did not understand it all, these events marked the turning point in Francis's life, moving him toward the transformation God had planned for him.

During that time Francis attempted to return to his life of strong drink, loud songs and beautiful women, but he found himself distracted and changed. He would awake from vivid dreams in which God was trying to lead him somewhere. While he prayed about it, he remained uncertain. One day, while walking in the country, Francis came upon the small, crumbling chapel of San Damiano, where he decided to pray. As he knelt before the crucifix and began to pray, he suddenly heard Christ speak to him from the cross before him: "Francis, Francis, go and repair My house which, as you can see, is falling into ruins."

Moved by the clarity and power of those words, he raced back to Assisi and sold all the fabric he could from his father's shop (as well as the horse he used to bring the fabric to a neighboring market), returning to San Damiano to present the money to the poor priest dedicated to the chapel's care. He even asked to move into the chapel to begin the task that God had given him: to repair his church. And so began the first of several restoration projects for neglected chapels throughout the countryside.

Years later Francis realized that God was not calling him to literally repair church buildings, though it was a very noble and godly act in itself. Rather, God had called him to repair the church, the body of Christ, which was falling into ruins through sin and compromise. He would eventually make the connection, but at first, God's words took him down an entirely different path. This story reminds us of Jesus' temptation in the wilderness and how the devil attempted to reinterpret God's words to lure Jesus into compromise.

SUBVERTING THE FAITHFUL

Just as it is important to read the Sermon on the Mount as a whole, respecting the wider context and direction of Jesus' teaching rather than reading it as a random collection of maxims, so too is it important that we place the Sermon itself into its proper context in the life of Christ. It is significant to both Jesus and us to understand what directly preceded the teaching of Matthew 5–7. By setting the stage we can better understand what Jesus is saying and what it means for us today.

The beginning of Matthew 4 finds Jesus making his way into the wilderness "to be tempted by the devil." Consider the contrast of this moment: having just been baptized by John, during which the Holy Spirit descended upon him like a dove and his heavenly Father declared, "This is my Son, whom I love; with him I am well pleased" (Matthew 3:17), Jesus immediately faces the enemy. And he faces him by himself in the wilderness, without even the most basic provisions for life and comfort. He is truly and completely alone. This is the price that sin demands, disconnecting us from God, each other and all of creation. And so, Jesus faces these temptations by himself. Cleverly, the devil does not attempt to seduce Jesus into blatant sinfulness—at least not as we so often understand sin. Rather, he employs the same tactics he used in the Garden of Eden (Genesis 3:1-5), twisting God's own words in an attempt to get Jesus to compromise his faithfulness.

Three times the devil tempts Jesus, but each time Jesus responds from Scripture, reaffirming the intentions and heart of God's words and his will for his Son. The enemy is not merely trying to get Jesus to "break a rule" here. In tempting Jesus in this way immediately after his baptism, we can see that the devil seeks primarily to subvert and compromise faithfulness to God. "The devil, a fallen angel, is the embodiment of the mystery of disobedience."[1] He is a mirror to our own impatience, our sinful desire for an easier way of obeying what God calls us to be and do. He reflects our own longing for cheap grace. It is in this way that the devil tempts us—alone, as individuals, disconnected from God's good creation through sin. Here the devil offers us a way to "solve" the problem of sin apart from God or others. It is an attractive lie, the temptation that has lured each of us again and again.

I know that these temptations are ever present in my own life and ministry, especially when we began our work in Winnipeg. When faced with the reality of living in an inner-city community, where all but one of my four immediate neighbors were drug dealers and pimps, I immediately began thinking of ways in which I could still follow God's calling but without so much personal risk.[2] A large camp facility was generously offered to us just outside the city as a place where we could offer retreats to inner-city kids, house a large staff with very little expense and still be able to commute to the inner city every day. Due to the challenges of living on the donations of family and friends, where we often only just made ends meet, the thought of pursuing a paid pastoral position became very appealing and readily available.

Ways that we could accomplish the task while reducing the difficulties and costs repeatedly came to mind—most completely legitimate in and of themselves. However, we knew that any such choice would be a compromise. The means was as important as the end. And so we made the choice to move into the old, abandoned gang house and become neighbors with gang bangers and prostitutes. Looking back, I am deeply grateful we made those choices.

COMMUNITY OF THE COMMITTED

Leaving the desert, having overcome the temptations of the devil and having been ministered to by the angels, Jesus returns to the world proclaiming his message of repentance and the costly kingdom of God. While he travels with this message, Jesus comes across the men who would become his closest companions and his devoted disciples. Encountering them in the midst of their daily work, Jesus calls them to follow him and employ their skills for God's kingdom, to "fish for people" (see Matthew 4:19). Amazingly, they follow him—immediately dropping what they are doing and following this new master.

From the solitude of the wilderness, Jesus emerges with a message that immediately forms community. And not just any community but a community of disciples, a community that requires formation and discipline. A community of apprentices who are being changed into faithful subjects of a new King and a new kingdom. Yet, with such a monumental purpose behind this community, Jesus astonishingly does not choose the spiritually elite or socially influential. Instead, consistent with his own humble nature, he surrounds himself with rough-around-the-edges common people. In what becomes a pattern throughout his life, Jesus is subverting the expectations of Israel regarding the nature of his kingdom.

Jesus' example here is a demanding one. His call for us to follow him is immediate and absolute. Just as he called his disciples amid their workplaces, so too he expects that we respond to his calling as our first priority. It is not enough to merely make room for Jesus in our lives, not enough to be volunteers in his mission when we have the time or the inclination. Rather, he calls us to follow him, to utilize all of our strengths, gifts and resources for our truest vocation—ambassadors of his emerging kingdom.

Just as Jesus emerged alone from the wilderness, so too he calls us out from the wilderness of our sin. He calls us out of the disintegrated isolation of sin, to die to *self*. This is not to say that individuality is an aspect of our sinfulness. Far from it! After all, he is a God who cares about every person, identifying with us as individuals—he is the God of Abraham, of Isaac and of Jacob. However, he ultimately calls us together. He calls us into a community so important to him, so precious, that he forms it as his very body. This community of the committed is a constant throughout Scripture, something we should be very mindful of in our individualistic age.

There are few topics I am more passionate about than community, and not just any community but the community of Christ, formed into his image for his mission. I have been deeply blessed to share life and ministry with some of the most unlikely but amazing women and men over the years. Beyond the romanticism that is often attached to community, we have lived together through the good, the bad and the downright ugly. We have seen each other at our most selfish and sinful moments. And it is precisely because of that messy reality that we are forced daily to have our hearts confronted by the cross. Slowly, day by day, our disintegrated selves decrease while Christ increases in and through our love for one another.

POWERFUL PROCLAMATION

With his community of committed disciples at his side, Jesus continues his ministry—teaching in the synagogues and proclaiming the gospel of the kingdom. More than that, he also miraculously begins to heal people of all manner of diseases and sicknesses. Inevitably, word spreads throughout the region and people flock to Jesus, bringing their sick with them. Before long, Jesus and his disciples can't go anywhere without huge crowds following them. We should not be too quick to see this early rise to fame as a mark of success. After all, these very people so eager to hear his words and receive his healing touch later cry out for him to be crucified. However, it is important to understand why these people pursued him.

Without question many were drawn by the power of his miracles. Who wouldn't want to see that? However, we often forget what healing meant to the Jewish people of Jesus' day. Like us, they would have longed for relief from their suffering and to be made whole again. More than that, though, many of those diseased, crippled and dying people were denied access to the temple, according to Old Testament law. In other words, by healing them Jesus not only relieves their physical suffering but restores their ability to enter into God's presence. What an act of revolutionary grace!

Not just Jesus' miracles but also his preaching drew people to him. Just as the physical and spiritual implications of his miracles are inseparable, so too are those works inseparable from the message he proclaimed. Proclaiming *and* living the gospel were tied together intrinsically. It is strange that today these two are held in such tension. In an attempt to push back against what is often seen (and often rightfully) as a trend toward reducing the gospel to only propositional truths, many Christians are fond of a quote attributed to St. Francis: "Preach the gospel at all times. When necessary, use words." But Francis never said this. In fact, Francis (like Jesus) preached wherever he went.

St. Francis never elevated action over speaking in the task of bringing the gospel to others, but neither did he believe that the gospel message was fully communicated only in words. Francis recognized that the gospel was the all-consuming work of God to restore all of creation to himself, for his glory. He embraced the truth that the power of the gospel proclaimed with his mouth was given authority by the Spirit-empowered life that reflected the reality of its transformation. Even in the imperfect, clumsy and often sinful lives that we lead, he knew that the inherent authority of the gospel message still touched the hearts of those who needed to hear it. Therefore it must be preached.

Allowing this dynamic tension to exist is critical for us at Little Flowers Community. We have learned very quickly that the poor, faced with the realities of their difficult lives, are able to spot hypocrites from a mile away. When our lives do not reflect the truth that we proclaim with our mouths, we sow seeds of mistrust and doubt in the hearts of those who hear us. God can and will work in spite of our failings, but we recognize that for our words to have authority we must actively seek to live them out as best we can, openly confessing and repenting of failures along the way. This tension is at the very heart of the Sermon on the Mount, so it should not surprise us that we see it practiced so blatantly right before Jesus teaches it.

HE BEGAN TO TEACH

The people are drawn to Jesus because they see in him an authority that is both unfamiliar and deeply compelling. Here is a man who lives the words he speaks, a man who proclaims a new kingdom with his words and then makes it possible, tangible and immediate with his actions. It is little wonder that Jesus and his disciples find themselves surrounded by crowds eagerly waiting to hear what he has to say. Leading them to the mountainside, Jesus sits in the posture of a teacher and begins to teach them.

Throughout the Gospel of Matthew the author goes out of his way to make sure his readers compare Jesus to Moses. For example, his recounting of Herod's massacre of the Jewish boys parallels the similar massacre at Moses' birth by the Egyptians. And just as Moses went up on Mount Sinai to receive the word of God (Exodus 19–20), Jesus also goes up a mountain. Jewish readers of this Gospel would have seen the startling implications: Matthew is linking the Sermon on the Mount to the Ten Commandments. The Ten Commandments are the moral foundation on which Jewish faith was built and sustained. They declare that the lord who delivered them from captivity is God. Jesus is the realization of that salvation, the one who leads us out of captivity to sin. Where Moses brought God's word carved on tablets of stone, Jesus came as the Word made flesh, dwelling among us.

When Moses went up the mountain into the presence of God, all others (except Aaron) would have been killed if they had tried to follow. Yet Jesus invites his followers with him to the mountain. Just as his healing miracles allowed the healed to more fuller enter into the presence of God, here he removes even more barriers (just as he did when he later welcomed the sick and lame into the temple after his triumphal entry into Jerusalem [Matthew 21:14]). Jesus himself surpasses both the Ten Commandments and Moses who brought them, for in him we see the fulfillment of all the Law and Prophets. While this truth might not have been fully evident to those listening to the Sermon on the Mount (though it was certainly implicit), Matthew's arrangement of the Gospel leaves little doubt for his readers. Any other reading would render his teaching impossible or even immoral.

> The Sermon on the Mount cannot help but become a law, an ethic, if what is taught is abstracted from the teacher. When the sermon is isolated from the one alone who is the exemplification of righteousness, it seems natural to ask if Jesus's teachings must be followed literally. Does Jesus really think it is possible to live without lust? How would we be able to run the world if we do not resist evildoers?[3]

Therefore, it is only because Jesus is the Word made flesh, truth incarnate, the Son of God and true Messiah, that we are able to truly live the words of his teaching in the Sermon on the Mount. More to the point, because of these facts we *must* live them, not by our own power and merit but by the grace of God and the power of his Holy Spirit in us:

> For through the law I died to the law so that I might live for God. I have been crucified with Christ and I no longer live, but Christ lives in me. The life I live in the body, I live by faith in the Son of God, who loved me and gave himself for me. I do not set aside the grace of God, for if righteousness could be gained through the law, Christ died for nothing! (Galatians 2:19-21)

Jesus, having faced and defeated the devil, overcoming all temptation in their first confrontation, went into the world proclaiming and embodying the good news of God's kingdom. He drew to himself a community—one whose bond surpassed familial devotion—to be formed into his image, his body, through discipleship and salvation. On this radical foundation, this startling claim of absolute authority, Jesus begins teaching the Sermon on the Mount: "Blessed are the poor in spirit . . ."

2

Blessed Are the Poor in Spirit

Matthew 5:3-12

After nearly eight hours of standing in the sun, Amy and I were beginning to act a little silly. We were both physically and emotionally exhausted so our conversation began to wander into all sorts of odd corners. Even the paramedics and police officers, who patiently waited with us on the street corner, joined in the quiet jesting. It was truly a surreal moment for all of us. What had brought us together, however, was far from a laughing matter. Our nervous chuckles covered the deep fear and uncertainty that hung over this unlikely and unfortunate event.

Living half a block away from us with her daughter and brother, Amy had been a part of our community long before we formally started Little Flowers as a small inner-city church. A single mom with a passion for Jesus, Amy is an evangelist through and through. Only weeks after her brother Andrew moved in with her, she shared with him the love and hope in Jesus Christ, which he gladly embraced. A truly gifted artist and all-around likable guy, Andrew also struggled from a rough childhood and untreated mental illness. He soon became a part of the Little Flowers family, his whole countenance changing for the better every day. It was beautiful to see and a privilege to be a part of.

Which is why I was unprepared for the call I received from Amy earlier that Mother's Day morning. Visiting her adoptive mother across town, Amy had received an emergency phone call from local police informing her that Andrew had jumped the fence into the construction site opposite their home, climbed several stories on the scaffolding and was threatening to jump. Since I lived seconds away from her house, she asked if I would go down there until she arrived. Grabbing my keys, cell phone and hat, I jogged the half block to where the police had already arrived en force.

Even though I already knew what I was walking into, my heart leapt into my throat as I watched Andrew sprint across the narrow, bouncing boards to the far end of the scaffolding high above my head. Throwing off the planks that made up the walkway, he cut himself off from all immediate access and leaned out over the edge, threatening to jump. It became very clear that he was terrified, confused and not himself. All I could do was pray, *God, help him.*

While Amy had arrived much earlier, when she attempted to talk to Andrew, he did not seem to know who she was, lost in a cloud of paranoia and confusion. So obvious was his rapid deterioration that his plight began to draw a crowd—neighbors, friends, even passersby stopped to watch the shocking scene they had encountered. One neighboring household even had a barbeque in their front yard so they could watch, their kids playing in full sight of the events. It is hard for me not to feel angry with such callous insensitivity, but perhaps, like so many of us, they found themselves facing the unimaginable with no sense of how to respond and therefore defaulted into the all-too-common pattern of our culture: voyeurism. For whatever reason, we were all captive with fear and dark anticipation.

And so we stood together, watching, waiting, hoping and praying. After those eight long hours had passed, we were sure it could only mean that he wasn't prepared to jump. However, just in case,

I positioned myself so that, while I could watch Andrew and keep Amy informed, she had her back to the scene and wouldn't see if anything happened. I do not know what inspired me to do that in that moment, but I can only believe that it was the Holy Spirit. Moments later, spreading his arms wide, Andrew leaped from the scaffolding and fell to his death. The instant he jumped, Amy saw the pain and disbelief on my face. As quickly as her brother's body had fallen to the ground, the grief came crashing down over her and she wept, repeating over and over: "No! No! Oh God, please, no!"

There, with Andrew's devastated sister sobbing into my chest, her fists clenched on my coat, I was overwhelmed by the gravity of what had just happened—the absolute, irreversible loss that Amy was experiencing, that all of us were experiencing. Death is never easy, but this was so tragic, so sudden and so violent, I had no words. All I could do was hold her and share her grief as best I could.

Blessed are those who mourn . . .

When faced with the stark reality of such unimaginable suffering, our carefully articulated theology, our quick spiritual platitudes and our easy assurances of salvation seem to crumble. And it was into this reality that God began to open up our hearts and minds and lives to the powerful and unrelenting truth of the Beatitudes. How, in light of such tangible loss and suffering, can we ever call ourselves blessed?

THE BLESSED

"Blessed are the poor." "Blessed are those who mourn." "Blessed are the meek."

These bizarrely paradoxical statements, too often rushed past with overfamiliarity, baffle us when we're confronted with hard realities such as extreme poverty, suicide and our culture of violence. Yet we cannot ignore that Jesus made these declarations as the defining and opening words of his powerful Sermon on the

Mount. In a day and age when the casual use of blessings is as common as sneezes, it is important that we understand what Jesus means by the word *blessed* in the Beatitudes. When we understand this key word, the truth of his teaching becomes that much more clear.

There are two words for "blessed" in Greek (corresponding with two Hebrew words with parallel meanings). The use of "blessed" that Christians are most used to hearing and using is the Greek *eulogeō*, which means to invoke or extend good wishes or intentions, such as "God bless you for all your hard work" or "Bless you for your faithfulness to Jesus." However, in the Beatitudes, Jesus does not use *eulogeō*, choosing instead to use the other word, *makarios*. As opposed to being an invocation for something we hope will happen to the subject of our blessing, this word is used to describe a current state of being, a *present* state of happiness and good fortune. "That is they affirm *a quality of spirituality that is already present*," affirms Ken Bailey, professor of Middle Eastern New Testament studies.[1]

In order to understand the Beatitudes, we must understand the critical differences between the meaning of these words for "blessed." If Jesus had used *eulogeō* instead of *makarios*, then the entire meaning of each verse would be dramatically changed. In fact, many Christians, unaware of the distinction that remains invisible in the English translation, continually apply the incorrect meaning to the word. If *blessed* was being used as an entreaty for good favor, then the Beatitudes could be understood as saying something like: "You've done well in your mourning; as a reward, you'll be comforted. Excellent job at being meek; as a gesture of my gratitude, you'll inherit the earth. You've got being poor in spirit down pat; therefore, this kingdom will be yours."

While inevitably we are called to live in ways consistent with the Beatitudes, Jesus is not offering a transaction of his favor in exchange for certain behaviors. Rather, he is describing a present reality of happiness in the midst of these various circumstances, be it poverty of spirit, mourning or meekness. In other words, the people described in the Beatitudes are fortunate in the here-and-now because they live in the assurance that God's promises are being fulfilled, in part in the present and in fullness in the future. God is not cutting deals with us or even making promises. Rather, he is describing the transformed reality of his kingdom as it breaks forth into the hearts and lives of his faithful people.

Why is this important? Reading the Beatitudes with the incorrect understanding can lead us into a false motivation where we pursue certain behaviors in order to reap the benefits listed. We do not simply tolerate being "poor in spirit" in the hope that we will be rewarded for it, but rather in the midst of our poverty of spirit we experience a blessing beyond our circumstances. Again, this is not to say that we should not seek to nurture hearts that reflect and produce the qualities listed in the Beatitudes, but Jesus is declaring that even now in seemingly hopeless circumstances his kingdom is secured for us and will someday come in its fullness.

With this understanding in place we can now dive into the Beatitudes.

THE POOR IN SPIRIT

The phrase "poor in spirit" has been a source of great debate throughout nearly all of church history. Was Jesus advocating poverty as a state of blessing? Is this a further affirmation that, like the rich young ruler, we must sell all we have and give to the poor in order to follow Jesus? St. Francis took Jesus quite literally in this respect—should we as well? Or is the inclusion of "in spirit" an indication that Jesus was talking about something more spiritual, relating instead to the attitudes of our hearts and not actual, material poverty? These questions and more continue to bring this text into debate.

An all-too-common misconception about these dynamics is that it is a binary choice of two opposing options, that it is referring only to material poverty or to spiritual poverty. This is too often the result of a false dichotomy that pervades our Western worldview, separating the "spiritual" world from the "material" one. Jesus and his followers, on the other hand, would have seen these two dynamics as inseparable aspects of a singular whole. Therefore, we must turn to both sides of the spectrum for understanding, examining the integrated whole of the spiritual and material reality.

When Jesus' disciples and the crowds heard him use this expression, it would most certainly have triggered immediate connections to several Old Testament texts they had heard all their lives. The expression was commonly used in their religious texts, prayers and other practices of faith. For example, in the face of their enemies and their own prideful negligence, the Jews knew full well the need for their humble dependence on God (Psalm 34:4-6; Zephaniah 3:12). The writings of the prophets, such as Isaiah 66:2, clearly expressed God's expectation that they live in humility and repentance:

> "Has not my hand made all these things,
>   and so they came into being?"
>   declares the LORD.

> "This is the one I esteem:
>   he who is humble and contrite in spirit,
>   and trembles at my word."

In the King James Version, the phrase used is "even to him that is poor and of a contrite spirit," making the connection between poverty and humility/contrition. Familiar though they were with this language, that this state of spiritual poverty was connected to inheritance in God's kingdom would have come as something of a shock to Jesus' listeners. The Jews were not strangers to God's kingdom breaking forth in times of trial or exile; however, previously their salvation in those cases had come through the defeat of their enemy and their subsequent liberation from bondage, most often after a time of communal repentance. Yet Jesus shifted the perspective. Instead of coming out of their bondage and into their inheritance, he declared that in the midst of their poverty they inherit his kingdom. In other words, liberty from the Romans did not seem to be on Jesus' immediate agenda. Further, what kind of a kingdom could be inaugurated while still under the subjugation of a godless empire? This was not the messianic revolution they were expecting.

Somehow, Jesus was inaugurating a kingdom in which the weak and the defeated were his blessed heirs. Those assumed to be the true heirs of God's favor were men like the Pharisees (religious laymen) and the Sadducees (priestly authorities), whose righteousness was certainly not characterized by humility and contrition, but strict adherence to the law.[2] While people grumbled at what they saw as collusion or compromise, many recognized that these religious men held influence and sway among their Roman overlords, thus providing some protection or at least a buffer. Surely they were the ones to inherit the kingdom. Instead, Jesus' words reflect a paradoxical shift in contrast to the expectations of the people. It is a foreshadowing of his words in Matthew 20:26-28: "Not so with you. Instead, whoever wants to become great among you must be your servant, and whoever wants to be first must be your slave—just as the Son of Man did not come to be served, but to serve, and to give his life as a ransom for many."

This pronouncement might have initially stirred some smug pleasure among the common people, all too eager to see these self-righteous men taken down a peg. However, as the implications began to sink in, those grins would have been short-lived. After all, if the commonly accepted categories of righteousness that kept the Pharisees in their positions of authority were dismantled,

Jesus' rearticulation left no room for anyone else to escape responsibility. Where one's acknowledged sin and inadequacy would have been an easy excuse for many to avoid living righteously in accordance to God's commands, that very brokenness was now ripe in its potential to produce humility and contrition, to bring forth the "poor in spirit."

Jesus was not inviting the poor to take pride in their poverty, as though their poverty was evidence of their righteousness. That would ultimately be making the same mistake as the Pharisees, but in reverse, where they believed their prosperity was evidence of their righteousness. Rather, Jesus was introducing a poverty that is neither accidental nor circumstantial, but that is an intentional relinquishment. If we make poverty an external commodity that we purchase our righteousness with, we lose sight of the inner transformation borne of the humility and contrition that God is truly seeking and nurturing in us.

Consider the beautiful words of the prophetic Magnificat:

My soul glorifies the Lord
    and my spirit rejoices in God my Savior,
for he has been mindful
    of the humble state of his servant.
From now on all generations will call me blessed,
    for the Mighty One has done great things for me—
    holy is his name.
His mercy extends to those who fear him,
    from generation to generation.
He has performed mighty deeds with his arm;
    he has scattered those who are proud in their inmost
        thoughts.
He has brought down rulers from their thrones
    but has lifted up the humble.
He has filled the hungry with good things

but has sent the rich away empty.
He has helped his servant Israel,
   remembering to be merciful
to Abraham and his descendants forever,
   even as he said to our fathers. (Luke 1:46-55)

Jesus isn't so much preaching the reversal of what Mary proclaimed, but an alternative foundation for justification, one of
contrition and humility as opposed to hyperpious triumphalism.
When Mary asserts explicitly that God is on the side of the poor,
we can understand it within the tension of what it means to be
blessed as the poor in spirit. Rather than elevating poverty to a
form of righteousness, Jesus is instead calling for a revolution of
imagination around the nature of what we consider true blessing.

Jesus is here declaring that the humble and repentant heart is
the fertile soil of his kingdom. Not a humility of false piety or
overexaggerated self-deprecation. Rather, a heart that knows its
dependence on God for forgiveness and restoration. A heart that
sees and acknowledges both the brokenness and the strengths
within it. It rejects the twin-faced pride of arrogance and self-
centered loathing. When we find ourselves in this place, where we
respond to God's grace in the light of our own sinfulness, *then* we
are already *in* the kingdom of God.

THE BONDAGE OF MATERIAL WEALTH

While this foundation of a humble and contrite heart is clearly
in place, Jesus could very well have made this clear without
using the language of poverty at all. The Greek word used for
"poor" is explicitly connected to material poverty. Was Jesus
using this word awkwardly, ignoring the potential confusion
such an association might cause? Of course not. The fact that
Jesus speaks about the challenges of material wealth more than
any other topic demonstrates that he would not have casually
used such language here or anywhere. It is clearly an intentional

use, and therefore we would be remiss in ignoring or minimizing it.

In his classic work *Christian Counter-Culture: The Message of the Sermon on the Mount*, John Stott affirms the overlapping meaning of this word. First, he demonstrates that the Old Testament concept of humility and contrition was born out of a dependency rooted in material need, adapting to the meaning we have just discussed.[3] Second, he recognized a pattern: "the rich tended to compromise with surrounding heathenism; it was the poor who remained faithful to God. So wealth and worldliness, poverty and godliness went together."[4] So, while being poor in spirit is acknowledging our spiritual bankruptcy before God, it includes a more holistic declaration of dependency than just an otherworldly need.

One of the most significant hints we have to this being Jesus' intentional meaning is the parallel verses found in Luke's Sermon on the Plain (Luke 6:20-26). In this text the list of four blessings in the Beatitudes is followed by a list of matching woes. Each blessing, then, is matched with an opposing woe, both contrasting and informing the meaning inherent in each. With this understanding, we can better understand Christ's intentions. In this case, the first beatitude in Luke 6 reads: "Blessed are you who are poor, for yours is the kingdom of God" (v. 20).

It should be noted here that while Luke clearly did not use "poor in spirit," this alone does not demonstrate that Jesus intended a material application (for the connection to humility and contrition would still have been assumed by the average Jewish listener). However, when we look at the matching woe in verse 24, it becomes clearer: "But woe to you who are rich, for you have already received your comfort."

With this understanding, we can then recognize that the first beatitude in Matthew's Gospel is speaking to more than just allegorical "poorness"; it is making an intentional connection to material wealth and poverty. However, the questions remain: What does Jesus mean? Is he really saying that it is a blessing to be poor?

ARE THE POOR REALLY BLESSED?

This dual meaning of what it means to be "poor in spirit" is all too often overlooked or minimized among Christians today, at least in more affluent cultural contexts. Focusing on the important aspects of humility and repentance, we often become too comfortable on that end of the spectrum, unaware of (or unwilling to see) the other side of its meaning and the implications for our own lives. It has been encouraging to see this trend shift in the church today, with an increased awareness of the material implications of Jesus' teaching. However, as we pursue this corrective path, we must be careful not to make the mistake of repeating the opposite extreme of that which we are seeking to change.

After more than fifteen years of missionary service, mostly in an inner-city context, one thing has become deadly clear to me: *poverty is no blessing.* Billions of people worldwide needlessly suffer and die because of the complex and far-reaching impact of poverty. Disease, exploitation, persecution, slavery, misogyny, murder and genocide flourish in contexts where the poorest of the poor reside. This suffering, a product of the sin that has corrupted all of creation, was never God's intention. In no way is Jesus saying that the dynamics of poverty are good. Rather, he is speaking of his capacity to redeem our suffering, to subvert the powers of sin and death for his glory through the power of his resurrection. The state of poverty can be an opportunity to engage in the redemptive freedom from other attachments, distractions and compromises that would otherwise so easily draw us away from God and his priorities.

Yet, throughout Christian history the tension between these two extremes has been difficult for the church to navigate. More often than not, when Christians fail in this respect, it is not the result of blatant disregard but rather out of a well-intentioned but misguided emphasis of one extreme over the other. Few of us could argue with the devastating and corrupting effect that consumerism and materialism has had on the church in our culture, predisposing us to minimize, ignore or even reject the material implications related to being "poor in spirit." However, we must also realize that as we seek to address this extreme, the opposite extreme has just as much potential to mislead us into dangerous territory.

Few examples better highlight the strengths and weaknesses of both sides of this spectrum than the life of St. Francis of Assisi. Specifically, Francis adopted the very severe vow of poverty. In the first expression of this vow, Francis and his followers rejected all personal property, with the exception of the rough habits they wore. The saint went so far as to forbid his followers from even touching money. Rather, they would trust God for their immediate provision of food and shelter through begging and working alongside the poor (with whom they generously shared). They were true mendicants—relying entirely on alms given to them by others to survive.

While Francis's literal adherence to this vow played no small part in the positive impact and authority he had in the church and wider culture of his day (and beyond), it is also quite clear that the extremity of his adherence was somewhat damaging as well. Even Francis, finding himself prematurely at the end of his life, repented to his suffering body for treating it so poorly. In the cold climate and harsh conditions, this vow left Francis literally blind and broken, leading to a death premature even by the standards of his day. Francis's commitment to this vow, however, was an expression of his passionate devotion to Christ and his attempt to live according to his teachings as literally as he could, seeking to find the blessings of the "poor in spirit."

Some have criticized Francis and his friars on this account. The pretense of their so-called voluntary poverty, it is charged, trivialized the involuntary poverty of the truly poor. Some argued that linking poverty to religious devotion provided an excuse for wealthy Christians to withhold charity and fail to confront systemic injustices that contributed to the very poverty they sought to relieve. Instead, they could view the poor as holy and their withholding of alms as a way of supporting the poor in their righteousness. Further, it is suggested that as a result of their popularity, much of the charitable giving that would otherwise have been given to the poor was instead given to the growing number of wandering friars.[5]

While such criticisms too often oversimplify the matter, their caution is well placed. With the rise in popularity among evangelical Christians of issues of social justice, and in such movements as "new monasticism" (where many choose to share life among the poor in the "abandoned places of the Empire"), how we relate to poverty is increasingly important.[6] For many of us, to be "poor in spirit" includes attempting to divest ourselves of our wealth, to identify with those on the margins. Like St. Francis, many of us—arguably most of us—who embrace lives of simplicity and service alongside the poor have done so voluntarily.[7] We choose to give up something of our wealth, be it finances, belongings or privilege (racial, gender, etc.). However, the very freedom to choose this kind of voluntary poverty is itself an expression of privilege. While this does not negate the value of such commitments, it should compel us to have a great deal more caution and intentionality as we seek to embrace this more holistic spiritual poverty.[8]

Rather than an affirmation of poverty, Jesus is exposing the dangers of wealth and privilege. This is a critical distinction because many passionate Christians are romanticizing poverty as they move toward lives of "service to the poor." By doing so they equate their "sacrifices" with noble gestures of love and self-denial for the sake of the poor whom they have come to save. In so doing, while embracing a form of external poverty, they fail to grasp humility and contrition on the other side of the spectrum. And for what should we be contrite and humbled? For many of us, our material, educational, familial and social privilege was inherited in part at the expense of others. Our participation in and failure to address the rampant materialism in our culture and in our churches indict us as well. Giving up wealth and privilege to share life among the poor is not done simply for the salvation of the poor but for the salvation of the rich (Luke 6:24). After all, if we are servants of the King in his kingdom, then all that we give (material or otherwise) is his anyway, for his purposes and glory, not our own. It is no credit to us to give to those in need that which is neither ours to begin with nor intended for us alone.

While extreme in his interpretation, St. Francis was not (as is often popularly suggested) primarily identifying with the poor in his embrace of the vow of poverty. Rather, Francis was attempting to identify (and imitate) Christ alone, whom he believed was also voluntarily poor. For Francis, the incarnation of Christ was the absolute act of humility and love. That Christ also lowered himself to identify with the poor was only natural and to be expected. Christ *was* the hungry, the thirsty, the stranger, the naked, the sick and imprisoned. Francis would have vehemently rejected any identification with the poor that was not first rooted in this primary identification with Christ, for without Jesus at the center it risked becoming mere activism and social posturing. Only in identifying with Christ could he have any true connection to his neighbor, both poor and rich.

When we grasp this understanding, the implications for all Christians are staggering. Whether you are called to live among the poor or not (and not everyone is called to move to the slums), all Christians are called to repent of the sin of greed and materialism, embracing sacrificial lives of radical generosity, hospitality and simplicity. For in following the example of Christ—identifying with him and his uncompromising commitment—we discover what it means to be truly "poor in spirit." It is only through identifying with Christ that we can begin to identify with the poor in meaningful and mutual ways.

THEIRS IS THE KINGDOM

As we saw earlier, Jesus' reference to God's kingdom would have had immediate meaning for a people living under the rule of a very different (namely, tyrannical) empire. The messianic expectations of the Jews were heightened by their current state of subjugation. Many of them were pining for their long-awaited Messiah to rise up and prove their identity as God's chosen people, casting out the pagan Romans at sword point. After all, how would they be a blessing to all the nations (and a curse to their enemies [Genesis 12:2-4]) if they were nothing but a dusty and distant province under the thumb of a ruthless foreign master?

Among the Jews of Jesus' day were many who actively pursued an armed response to the Roman invaders. These Zealots (stemming from a Hebrew word meaning "zealous on behalf of God") were passionate and often violent adherents to one Ruler, one Lord—God alone. They sought to forcefully subvert and resist the power of the Roman Empire, often acting out even against other Jews who they felt were collaborators. Fueled by tales of Old Testament military victories over their enemies through the power of God, these zealous warriors were determined to bring about God's just kingdom through their swords. While the Zealots were not yet widely organized, and only representative of a smaller segment of the Jewish people, many held deep sympathy for this group's ideals, longing for them to rise up on their behalf. These were the people who were expected to take the kingdom.

And yet Jesus describes his coming kingdom as the inheritance of the poor and the empty. It is significant that this entire teaching opens with this beatitude, making clear from the very beginning something critical about this emerging kingdom, its citizens and the King who reigns over it. The kingdom of God is characterized and inherited by those who humble themselves in repentance and choose to empty themselves of any attachments, whether in their hearts or their pockets. Against our natural ambition for position and power, Jesus promises his kingdom to the downwardly mobile, to those who follow his example and empty themselves, becoming instead servants (Philippians 2:5-8).

The kingdom is not to be established by force (the Zealots), nor is the kingdom a reward for the unbroken insider (the Pharisees); it is a covenant promise of God to the poor in spirit, an alchemical reaction to poverty of spirit and openness to the visitation of God.

Just as the kingdom would not come through those like the Pharisees in positions of social influence (nor through our own positions as politically engaged citizens of our nations), neither would it be brought about through the violent insurrection of the Zealots (nor by our economic or military might today). Rather, it will be the "publicans and prostitutes, the rejects of human society, who knew they were so poor they could offer nothing and achieve nothing. All they could do was to cry to God for mercy."[9] For it was precisely their lack of pretense that exposed the universal dependency of all people on God, a dependency all too often hidden from the wealthy and privileged who rely on their own means instead of God.

In the Gospels Jesus refers to the kingdom in many ways. Among them, he says that the kingdom, while a future promise in its fullness, is a present reality in the lives of his followers. As the Lord's Prayer teaches, our priority as believers is to seek his kingdom— that is, to participate in this kingdom that is breaking through into our current, present reality. Inherent in this affirmation of the poor in spirit is an active participation in the mission of God in the world. Out of this kingdom declaration of the first beatitude, all other beatitudes are birthed and given context and meaning.

WHAT DOES THIS MEAN FOR US?

As Little Flowers Community began our journey of exploring and embracing the teachings of the Sermon on the Mount, this first beatitude was significant. Because our neighborhood is a high-risk inner-city community, with many of our own members struggling with poverty in various forms, it was not difficult for us to understand the material implications of being "poor in spirit." But not because we embrace some romantic ideal that poverty makes people somehow predisposed to righteousness. Far from it! Many of the poor we have come to know and call friends in our years of ministry would rob you blind given the opportunity. Rather, poverty often strips away the pretense that wealth and privilege provide, exposing our universal brokenness and sinful nature. More often than not with the poor, what you see is what you get.

However, not every Christian lives in such an inner-city context. Not every Christian community is in proximity to the kind of poverty we see every day. While I would never suggest that all Christians should abandon the rural and suburban neighborhoods they call home and join us in the so-called slums, I am deeply concerned that our lives are too easily isolated from the realities of poverty, both locally and globally. The way we live in relation to both poverty and wealth must suffer the intense scrutiny Scripture demands, and then we must make the necessary changes to our lives. After all, when God said to his people that "there should be no poor among you" (Deuteronomy 15:4), he wasn't suggesting segregation.

If we attempt to merely apply these lessons as principles that can be attached to our current lives of faith, we will surely fail. The implications of this teaching on every aspect of life are staggering. If we truly embrace a poverty of spirit in which we pursue humility and genuine repentance, it will invariably force us to examine every aspect of how we live, as individuals, families and communities of faith, demanding repentance and active change whenever necessary. This first beatitude calls us to "follow Jesus through the eye of the needle."

That phrase is the title of a book by my friend Kent Annan, whose commitment to live out this beatitude led him and his wife into a life of service and solidarity with the poor of Haiti.[10] Already devastated by poverty, corruption, and the deep scars of slavery and racial tension, Haiti was rocked in January 2010 with a massive earthquake, plunging the nation further into hopeless despair. For Kent, asking those difficult questions led him to a life of genuine risk, great cost and insurmountable odds. Visiting Haiti with Kent a few months after the quake, surrounded by what could only be described as a war zone, I was humbled and challenged by the example of the Haitian Christians I met. Here is a people who, already suffering under poverty, had lost everything in a trauma so great that it would define an entire generation. And yet their selfless commitment to each other and their incredible hospitality reflected Christ in a way I have rarely encountered in my own wealthy nation. In the midst of the truest poverty, they are living in the kingdom of God.

Later in the Sermon on the Mount Jesus makes this even more clear: "Do not store up for yourselves treasures on earth, where moth and rust destroy, and where thieves break in and steal. But store up for yourselves treasures in heaven, where moth and rust do not destroy, and where thieves do not break in and steal" (Matthew 6:19-20).

The lesson of this first beatitude makes demands of the rich and poor alike. For the wealthy (the category most of us belong to), it requires that we live counterculturally in a world where material wealth is the unquestioned ideal, embracing a life of radical generosity and of absolute dependence on God and his people. Not even material security can be a first priority. For the poor (and this is a lesson that I hesitate to share out of my own position of wealth and privilege), it requires embracing a sufficiency in Christ that, while not ignoring or blindly accepting the injustices and sufferings of poverty, does not seek reparations by pursuing and embracing the empty promises of materialism and privilege. All of us must seek to live in such a way that in all things we will decrease so that Christ might increase.

Blessed Are the
Mourners and the Meek

Matthew 5:4-5

Within seven months of watching Andrew take his own life, two other friends of mine also chose suicide in the face of their brokenness and pain. It was a year filled with mourning like I have never experienced before. While all death is tragic, the wide-ranging effects of suicide leave devastation in its wake. Family and friends are crippled with questions, fears and uncertainties. *Could we have done more? How could we have missed the signs? Is it somehow our fault?* It is not surprising that when people intentionally take their own lives, it quite often triggers the same impulse in others. It is difficult to consider the state of being in mourning as a possible blessing.

To further underline this seemingly nonsensical commendation of mourning, we also live in a world that makes our happiness and comfort of prime importance. No one wants to mourn if they don't have to; no one feels lucky to have the chance to grieve and weep. The sackcloth and ashes of biblical mourning have long since been exchanged for stylish black suits and modest but flattering dresses, followed by finger food and quiet conversation. We consider ourselves blessed if we can go home early without the discomfort of facing the difficult emotions, the unanswered questions and the suffering of others. So what could Jesus have possibly meant when he called the mourner blessed?

> Blessed are those who mourn,
>> for they will be comforted. (Matthew 5:4)

In the midst of this contrast the answer reveals itself to us. Jesus' life, and the life he calls us to, stands in stark and intentional contrast to the way of the world. Like all the Beatitudes (as in the whole Sermon on the Mount), this truth can only be understood as it is seen as an expression of who Jesus is. Philippians 2:5-8 says:

> Your attitude should be the same as that of Christ Jesus:
>
> Who, being in very nature God,
>> did not consider equality with God something to be
>>> grasped,
> but made himself nothing,
>> taking the very nature of a servant,
>> being made in human likeness.
> And being found in appearance as a man,
>> he humbled himself
>> and became obedient to death—
>>> even death on a cross!

Jesus put aside his rights, his power and his privilege, and became one of us in order to bring us the hope of salvation. He set aside the pursuit of the happiness and joy the world offers, instead choosing the costly life of the cross for our sake. As we, in following him, renounce worldly happiness, we know that we will find ourselves in the company of those who mourn. We mourn for the world, with its empty promises of power, prosperity and passion. We mourn for our own natures that have pursued (and continue to long for) these shallow substitutes of God's true blessings. We mourn with those who suffer pain, both self-inflicted and caused by others. And we are blessed in our mourning, because we are sharing in the mourning of Christ, who wept over Jerusalem, who wept at Lazarus's tomb, who weeps for the sin and brokenness of the world, including our own. We are blessed because we know our mourning is not in vain, for we know we will receive comfort.

FOR THEY SHALL BE COMFORTED

When St. Francis and his followers began to live out the calling they believed God had placed on their lives, they surprised many by their course of action. Rather than withdrawing from the world into a rural, cloistered life of prayer and contemplation like the Benedictines (though they deeply respected the Benedictines and owe a great deal to them for the survival of their own order), they chose to live in the cities among the people, especially the poor. Refusing to own any property, they relied entirely on the generosity and hospitality of others. When food or shelter was not available, they relied on the provision of nature and slept under the stars. This is why the Franciscan tradition is more commonly referred to as a mendicant order (meaning they relied entirely on begging).

While such self-denial was not uncommon among other mendicant groups, Francis and his followers distinguished themselves in the nature of their mendicancy. Unlike other groups, the Franciscans did not embrace this radical lifestyle out of the conviction that the things they abstained from were evil. Rather, it was the example of Jesus himself that inspired such devotion. Francis was deeply moved by God's willingness to condescend out of love to become a man, and even then as one of the least—a man of questionable birth, from a rejected community, of a people under the rule of an enemy, living among the social and spiritual outcasts. Francis interpreted Jesus' lifestyle as one of voluntary poverty in order to live in loving solidarity with the poor. Though taken to extremes at times, this radical devotion to following the footsteps of the incarnated Christ was central to the impact of Francis and the Franciscan movement on church (and world) history.

This commitment to be meaningfully and sacrificially present with each other in our brokenness is born out of the example of Jesus Christ's incarnational presence in the world. In *The Message*, Eugene Peterson translates John 1:14 as saying, "The Word became flesh and blood, and moved into the neighborhood."

Francis believed that when Christians were referred to as the body of Christ in Scripture, it meant that they were called to live together as Christ, living as he would in their communities and in the world. And just as Christ lowered himself to share in the brokenness and grief of humanity in order to bring us hope and salvation, so too are we called to enter into the lives of our neighbors— brokenness and all—and share the hope and salvation that we have found in the midst of our own suffering.

Years ago, while participating in a canoe trip as part of a Christian teen camp, I sat around a campfire with a dozen or so young people. Several of the campers began to share their darkest fears and most secret wounds. One of the older teens, attempting to share his own sense of being unlovable, began to cry. We all stared uncomfortably at the fire as his sobs filled the nighttime silence. Someone needed to say something! It was then that one of the leaders moved over to sit next to him. He placed his arm around the young man's shoulders and then began to weep. Shocked, the teen turned to him and asked him what was wrong, to which the leader answered between breaths: "I am crying with you!" At these words, the young man fell into his arms and they wept. So did I and several others.

All too often, when faced with the sadness and suffering of others, we rush to offer comfort in order to ease our own discomfort. While we are no doubt motivated by good intentions, too often we hope to relieve the awkwardness and rawness of the other's suffering. We want to give advice, to solve the problem, to fix what is broken as much to relieve our own discomfort as to genuinely help the other's hurt. Instead, Jesus invites us to come alongside, identify with those suffering and join them in their mourning.

The Jews who were listening to Jesus preach were well acquainted with suffering and mourning. They lived under the thumb of an oppressive foreign power that committed untold injustices against them. Even their own religious and political leaders failed to stand up for them in the face of such blatant suffering. When Jesus said "Blessed are those who mourn," I expect many longed for him to finish the sentence with, "for they shall be vindicated!" How else could they find any sense of blessing in the midst of their suffering and mourning? Yet Jesus does not offer vindication but rather extends comfort.

The community into which Jesus invites us is beautiful because it is a sacred place—the only place—in which the mourner can truly find comfort. In this community our repentance is born out of our shared confession and forgiveness; here our mutual brokenness does not expose us but rather unites us in grace. It is a place where our suffering, whether at the hands of others or by tragic circumstance, can find relief, a sanctuary of hope and compassion. When we encounter the radical grace of the community formed in Christ, we are compelled to share it with others, to invite them into our brokenness to therefore share in our comfort. To mourn is not a denial of Christ's ultimate victory over suffering, but rather the natural and appropriate response to a world in which we have been separated from our Creator. And as we mourn, we are comforted by his Holy Spirit, the great Comforter who dwells in and among us, uniting us as his body.

The promise of a loving God choosing to comfort us even as we mourn our very betrayal of him is an act of startlingly radical grace. We must face the reality that this kind of radical grace means extending comfort to those seen as the least desirable people in our society. As a teenager I remember overhearing a group of Christian adults discuss the Oklahoma City bombing. Understandably, they were deeply upset by the events. Someone commented that the bombers deserved to suffer for what they had done. In truth, they did deserve to suffer great punishment for their horrible crime. Yet I found myself confronted by the uncomfortable truth that I deserve no better. The grace I receive from God is no more deserved by me than by those who perpetrated that awful deed. Our desire for retribution and vengeance might well be justified, but by affirming these desires we expose ourselves to equal judgment. And so God, in his infinite grace, mercy and love, chooses to suspend his judgment and instead promises us his comfort. How, then, can we do any less for each other?

And yet we so often fail to extend to others what we have so freely and undeservedly received ourselves. After all, what would the world think if we did? While some would see and embrace the beauty and hope of such love, others would inevitably reject it as offensive. Sitting across from a friend who had just beaten his girlfriend in a fit of frustrated rage, I am not proud to say that I was tempted to give him a taste of his own medicine. His pleas of contrition sounded empty to me. But as I recognized my own sinful brokenness and saw past the hypocrisy of my judgment, I saw in his tear-filled eyes a desperate longing to be free of his anger and a deep shame for what he allowed it to produce in his life. So I placed my arm over his shoulder and mourned with him, inviting the only One capable of bringing healing into such sorrow. And we were both comforted.

Christ's call for us to mourn together in the face of sin and suffering is a humble declaration of our own brokenness. This humanizing admission of our absolutely mutual and common fallenness should subvert our impulse to seek vengeance and retribution, moving us instead to comfort one another in the only true hope—

that which we find in the undeserved and undiscriminating grace of Jesus Christ. This same Christ, who alone claims the right of judgment over us all, comes first and foremost with longsuffering love and forgiveness.

As Amy and I returned to my house after praying together over Andrew's broken body at the hospital emergency room, only minutes after he was declared dead, we found the house far from empty. In the hours of waiting before he jumped, calls were made and the community had gathered. When she stepped into the front door of our home, Amy was greeted with the arms and tears of a group of friends who love her and would mourn with her. We ordered pizzas and sat around together, comforting each other as the waves of emotions and questions swelled throughout the evening. That night, as Amy and her daughter moved in with us for support, so too did several other people from Little Flowers Community. For nearly a week, we lived and mourned together under the same roof.

For that week we lived in the paradox of Ecclesiastes 7:1-4:

> A good name is better than fine perfume,
>   and the day of death better than the day of birth.
> It is better to go to a house of mourning
>   than to go to a house of feasting,
> for death is the destiny of every man;
>   the living should take this to heart.
> Sorrow is better than laughter,
>   because a sad face is good for the heart.
> The heart of the wise is in the house of mourning,
>   but the heart of fools is in the house of pleasure.

In our imperfect way we came together to mourn the brokenness in all of us that had found expression in such a terrible loss. And yet in our mutual comfort we also discovered the very present reality of the true Comforter in our midst, who promised a hope that surpassed even this great tragedy. We were blessed in our mourning, for we were truly comforted.

BLESSED ARE THE MEEK

The next beatitude Jesus proclaimed seemed to anticipate the resistance he would face in the previous one.

> Blessed are the meek,
>> for they will inherit the earth. (Matthew 5:5)

After all, as the people began to look increasingly to Jesus as the promised Messiah, they were hopeful that he would bring with him immediate and fierce justice, namely, the defeat of their pagan oppressors. If Jesus' emphasis on comfort over vindication was missed or ignored by the people, his declaration of "blessed are the meek, for they will inherit the earth" was a clear challenge to their militant expectations. Jesus was again presenting a far different kingdom that demanded a far higher price.

To understand this beatitude we must first look at two words. First, what does Jesus mean by "meek"? To most of us, to be meek means to be docile, tame, submissive, passive and even weak. Was Jesus truly saying that those without enough courage or strength to stand up for themselves would be blessed? Of course not! What then did he mean? How is it that we have come to understand meekness in such a derisive way?

To better understand Jesus' words, we look to the Old Testament, to the sacred texts he and his listeners had been raised with. The words of Psalm 37 would surely have come to many of their minds upon hearing Jesus' teaching. Verse 11 says, "But the meek will inherit the land and enjoy great peace."[1] However, the verses leading up to this are quite telling:

> Do not fret because of those who are evil
>> or be envious of those who do wrong;
> for like the grass they will soon wither,

like green plants they will soon die away.

Trust in the LORD and do good;
  dwell in the land and enjoy safe pasture.
Take delight in the LORD
  and he will give you the desires of your heart.

Commit your way to the LORD;
  trust in him and he will do this:
He will make your righteous reward shine like the dawn,
  your vindication like the noonday sun.

Be still before the LORD
  and wait patiently for him;
do not fret when people succeed in their ways,
  when they carry out their wicked schemes.

Refrain from anger and turn from wrath;
  do not fret—it leads only to evil.
For those who are evil will be destroyed,
  but those who hope in the LORD will inherit the land.

A little while, and the wicked will be no more;
  though you look for them, they will not be found.
But the meek will inherit the land
  and enjoy peace and prosperity. (vv. 1-11 NIV 2011)

Here we are admonished not to envy the evildoers and pleasure seekers. However, it is not a cautionary tale against the dangers of sin but rather an almost sympathetic revelation of the ultimate emptiness of their shallow pursuits. God is not calling us to be cowed in fear but rather to practice humility, restraint and to put our trust entirely in him. Only then will we enjoy true peace and prosperity.

The second critical word that we must understand in this beatitude is *earth*. Reading this, most of us would assume Jesus is talking about *planet* earth, the world. Yet looking back at Psalm 37, we see that Jesus is referring rather to "the land," specifically to the land of promise (or Promised Land), the culmination of so much of the Israelites' history and covenant with God. While the word *earth* might be appropriate insofar as all nations would be blessed through God's people (which is implicit in the Abrahamic covenant), the central exhortation of Jesus in this verse is to humility, obedience and peace. Consider how this would have sounded to a people living under the rule of the pagan empire of Rome.

It is hard for most of us to imagine what life under such a regime would be like. Not only were they robbed of their political and economic freedoms, but the very fabric of the people, the very defining story of who they were—chosen especially by God—was rejected, degraded and despised. Their only hope was that God's chosen and anointed One would rise up and lead them into the fullness of God's covenant with them, making them great among the nations. This man, Jesus, seemed to be the best hope they had found in some time and many eagerly longed for him to make his move and overthrow the Romans in a show of God-ordained authority and power.

Yet Jesus did no such thing. In fact, Jesus declared that those who will truly inherit the land of promise and all that God's covenant entails would be characterized by the tempered and humbled zeal of the meek. *The meek?* How in the world were the meek going to claim the land? Sure, the self-control and faithfulness of those who refused to be drawn into conflict by their enemies were worthy of respect. Those people were even to be admired! But surely they would not be the ones to whom the Jews' final liberty could be entrusted. Yet this was exactly what Jesus promised.

Jesus was again subverting their expectations that they would see the liberation of their Promised Land through a show of superior might and strength. While humble obedience to God was, on its own, by no means a controversial command, that he made their inheritance of the Promised Land (and with it all the covenant promises of God) contingent on obedience would have felt like a crippling blow to their hope for liberation. How would anything short of rising up with the Spirit and the sword free them from the profane mastery of Rome? It is a question that the church still wrestles with. Jesus' answer seems like foolishness (1 Corinthians 1:27) in light of the world we live in.

St. Francis took this call to humility and peace very seriously. Once a soldier with dreams of glorious military victory for God and kingdom, Francis slowly became convinced that the hope and promises of Christ could not be fulfilled by the sword (planting the seed for the developing Franciscan pacifism). In 1219 he and few companions set out on a journey to Egypt, where the battle lines of the fifth crusade were fiercely drawn. Seeing the devastation that war was having on both sides, Francis crossed enemy lines to plead with the Muslim sultan Malik al-Kamil. His logic was simple: if he could convert the sultan to Christianity, he could help bring about peace. With a price for the head of every Christian having been issued by the sultan, Francis and his companions knew it was a mission that would likely lead to their martyrdom.

Indeed, Francis was captured, beaten and brought before the sultan for judgment. There, with humility and confidence, Francis proclaimed the gospel of Christ, extolling the virtues of love and peace. So impressed was the sultan with Francis's passion, matched only by his humility, that he spared his life, offering him great wealth and riches as a reward. Committed to his vow of poverty, Francis further impressed al-Kamil by graciously refusing the riches. Unlike any Christian the sultan had met before, Francis embodied Christ with a prophetic authority and a simple humility that left a lasting impression.[2] While failing to convert the Muslims (unfortunately and needlessly violating countless cultural courtesies and protocols in the process), Francis planted a seed of peace and truth that flourished for generations.

When Jesus declares that those who are humbly submitted to God are blessed, he is not referring to a quiet, reserved, disempowered people. Rather, he is pointing to a people who, like Francis, resist their violent impulses for vengeance and retribution and follow the radically risky and sacredly foolish path of peace and love. Who could look at Francis's example in this story as anything but bold, courageous, selfless and obedient? Further, rather than defying the sultan in the face of inevitable martyrdom, he confidently proclaimed the gospel of the grace and love of Jesus. This poor little holy man made it very clear whose example he followed in embodying this "meekness": he followed the very humility and grace shown by the King of kings, Jesus Christ.

The realization of our poverty of spirit brings us to genuine repentance and mourning before God. Only as we repent of our sinfulness and acknowledge our dependence on God can we truly submit ourselves in genuine humility to obediently live as he teaches us. It is not that we seek to be meek in order to earn the reward of the inheritance, but rather that we are truly blessed because such humble obedience is only possible through Christ by his Spirit for the glory of the Father. In other words, without Christ, we have no hope of being meek or coming into the covenant promises.

The neighborhood in which Little Flowers Community has set its roots is by no means as dangerous as the fierce battleground of a thirteenth-century crusade. However, choosing to make it our home has been a continual act of humbling submission when the world would suggest a far different course of action. For those of us who moved into the neighborhood, it has been a willingness to give up the privilege and security of the familiar (too often the fruit of historic and present injustice) for the relative costs and dangers of an inner-city community. For those who already called it home, it has been a willingness to give up their right for a "better life in a better neighborhood" in order to participate in the emergence of God's kingdom in the midst of the West End.

For each one of us and the communities we are members of, we must realize and accept that humble obedience to Christ always costs us something, usually dearly. The way of Jesus, without exception, calls us to live apart from and against the ways of the world—a way of life that will invariably be costly, dangerous, and even the cause of societal (or even familial) alienation and rejection. If our lives fail to reflect this costly obedience, it must serve as a red flag of warning that we are living outside of the will of God. After all, the way of Christ must by necessity lead to the cross, and it does so daily.

Lord, have mercy. Christ, have mercy.

Blessed Are the Justice Cravers, the Merciful and the Pure in Heart

Matthew 5:6-8

Due to his increasing renown as a holy man, whose order was given permission to form by the Holy Father, Pope Innocent III himself, St. Francis of Assisi was soon welcomed by the poor and the rich alike. While he lived a life of voluntary poverty among the many poor people in the land, he was also occasionally invited into the homes of the wealthy and influential. Wanting to honor this saint-to-be, these hosts would offer Francis fine meals of choice meats and good wine. With expressions of great gratitude, Francis would bless the food and pull up to eat. However, before digging in, Francis would reach into his dirty tunic and withdraw his own special spice: a small bag of ashes which he would sprinkle over all his food.

Why would Francis do such a thing? He couldn't be accused of wasting the food, as he would promptly eat every ash-covered bite, but why spoil so generous a meal? Francis's actions here can be understood as part of his commitment to the *mortification of*

the flesh—that is, self-imposed denial and even physical punishment to attain a higher, more spiritual reward through suffering,
which was common among the monastic orders. Unlike many
others, however, Francis did not seem to embrace these sacrifices
primarily to denounce the evils of "fleshly pleasures," for he joy-
ously affirmed the goodness in God's creation. Neither was he
seeking to barter with God by giving up the good pleasures of life
in order to be rewarded. Rather, Francis sought to free himself
from any craving that might distract from his primary hunger for
God and his kingdom.

As mentioned in the introduction, St. Francis would later regret
the severity of this commitment, repenting to his devastated body
for such ruthless treatment. However, despite the extremes he
went to in pursuit of this devotion, we can see in Francis's actions
a deep understanding of what it means to "hunger and thirst for
righteousness." Francis understood that the multitude of cravings
and desires that bombard us compete daily for our attention and
devotion. He knew that the single-minded loyalty that Christ expected of his followers would not—*could not*—be shared with any
other desire.

Laura understands this truth better than most. When Laura
started coming to Little Flowers Community, it was immediately
clear that she would fit in. Eccentric, boisterous and passionate
about Jesus, she quickly became part of the fabric of the group.
Having recently moved to the city for work, she was quickly rising
in the ranks with her employer, proving her strong leadership and
managerial gifts. Those strengths were soon put to work in our
community as well, which was a great blessing for us all.

However, I began to suspect something was wrong when I heard
stories of Laura's financial challenges. I knew she was making a
better wage than most people in the community, so I was curious
about the source of her troubles. At first, it seemed as though it
might be the typical debts and expenses that often pile up, but

even that did not add up. Then one day Laura called, wondering if we could talk. It turned out that Laura had an addiction. As addiction is fairly common in our neighborhood, with friends and housemates struggling with drugs and alcohol abuse, her explanation made sense. "What are you addicted to?" I asked her. Her answer: shopping.

It might have been easy for me to downplay or dismiss a shopping addiction in the face of the other more illicit addictions I saw every day. However, it was clear that she was in the grip of something that she could not overcome alone, which was systematically dragging her into debt, despair and depression. Let me take this moment to tell you that this addiction is very real and very devastating. It is all too easy to minimize it or even make it the butt of casual joking. But this addiction is an increasing problem in our culture that needs to be taken seriously. With the help of the community, Laura is choosing to confront her addiction and begin the lifelong and daily journey of resisting those impulses. She has been an inspiration to me in her ruthless perseverance.

One of the most beautiful and exciting results of Laura's battle against this addiction is that, as she resists the cravings for material things, her heart has begun to be filled increasingly with a new hunger—a deep, almost desperate hunger to see God's kingdom come alive in her own life and in our community. She discovered, like Francis, that as we put down the selfish desires that consume us (and that push us to consume), our hearts begin to fill with God's cravings and his will. Against the grain of expectations and what is considered normal, Laura asked us to hold her credit cards to help her resist impulse purchasing. She asked us to check with her regularly, asking the hard questions, not only about her cravings to shop but the stresses that led to such cravings. She chose to alter her life in such a way as to disrupt her own misguided longings in order to nurture her longing for God. While Laura continues the process of finding freedom from her addic-

tion, she continues to persevere in pursuit of God's kingdom and
his righteousness.

> Blessed are those who hunger and thirst for righteousness,
>   for they will be filled. (Matthew 5:6)

We don't have to be addicts to see the universal truth in this
dynamic. It is quite difficult for us to talk about genuine hunger or
thirst from a place where most of us have never truly been without. Unlike those listening to Jesus' words, few of us have truly
known what it means to go without the basic needs for survival.
We live in a culture of sickening consumption and self-indulgence,
that masks the starvation of our souls by filling us up with things
that will never satisfy but keep us from realizing our desperate
need for the true Bread of life.

Before we can even begin to hope to hunger and thirst for righteousness, we must ruthlessly confront these other hungers that
we indulge so uncritically. This is why the Beatitudes cannot be
taken as stand-alone maxims or ideals, but must be seen together
as a movement toward Christ. Only when we embrace our brokenness and poverty of spirit can we repent with genuine remorse.
Only through such contrition can we become truly humble and
willing. And here, in this humbled state of willing repentance, we
are ready to be filled with the hunger for God's righteousness. To
long for this means to do so to the exclusion of all other longings.
Our devotion must be single-minded and absolute.

But what is this righteousness? The word *righteousness* carries
a lot of baggage. After all, who can stand the self-satisfied smug-
ness of the holier-than-thou, the *self*-righteous? Here is an example of where our translations fail to reflect the beautiful, nuanced
meaning of the Hebrew and Greek words in Scripture. Writer and
theologian John Driver sums it up well:

> In short, righteousness describes the quality of relation-
> ships which characterizes life together in the kingdom. In

the Gospel of Matthew righteousness often means a good relationship with God which is attained by means of submission to his will. In the context of the Sermon on the Mount it is transparently clear that God's will implies ordering one's life according to the values embodied in Jesus' teachings.[1]

Here we see a righteousness made manifest in an active and relational devotion to God that overflows into our relationships with others as well. In the Old and New Testaments, the fullness of God's will, as expressed in the Law and the Prophets, comes down to loving God and loving others (Matthew 22:36-40).[2] This connection between our right relationship with God and our right relationships with others is why many scholars suggest that the word *righteousness* in this verse might better be translated as "justice." True righteousness, then, in addition to drawing us more deeply into our devotion and service to God, bears fruit in active service, mercy and love to others.

Many of the Jews listening to Jesus' teaching presumed, as do many of us today, that the works of righteousness they were called to were the moral and religious obligations that had to be fulfilled according to the letter of the law. By linking such righteousness to the idea of hunger and thirst, Jesus subverts this subservience to the law, transforming it into a willing and fervent desire. True righteousness then, while proven by external acts of justice, is born out of a heart transformed by loving, willing devotion to Christ. True justice is born of love.

FOR THEY WILL BE SATISFIED

I wonder what the people thought of Jesus' words. When they considered their longing for justice, again, I can only imagine that thoughts of vindication against their Roman occupiers would have been at the top of their list. They would have loved to hear Jesus declare, "Blessed are those who rise up against injustice, for they will be victorious!" Instead, he promised that if their poor, contrite and humbled hearts longed for God's righteousness, their longing would be fulfilled. The fulfillment of that longing, then, would not come through some military defeat of their external enemy but through the conquering of the true enemy, their sinful nature. And if their enemy was not Rome, then their satisfaction would be a very different kind of liberation. Vindication will come, but in keeping with Jesus' pattern, it defies the expectations of the Jews, as it so often does our own.

Just as our "daily bread" mentioned in the Lord's Prayer comes only after our commitment to his kingdom and submission to his will, this beatitude reminds us that our true fulfillment, even before basic material survival, comes through God's just kingdom and righteous will. He is calling us to a passionate longing for this kingdom above all else, as though our very survival depends on it, because, in point of fact, it does.

Jesus is not, however, unsympathetic to the very real needs of our material survival. The word *satisfied* used here is the same Greek word used in the miracles of the loaves and fishes, which describes the crowds as having eaten their fill and being "satisfied" (Matthew 14:20; 15:37). As God's justice reflects a kingdom where people live in peace, health and right relationship, this promised satisfaction also includes our "daily bread." We can be secure in the promise of his provision as we live justly and righteously in the world. After all, how can we expect God to provide for the hungry poor when we squander our wealth on selfish desires or participate in systems—economic, social, political or spiritual—that profit at the expense of others? To hunger for justice is to examine our entire lives against the measure of Christ. Consider the words of the psalmist:

> Rise up, O LORD, confront them, bring them down;
>   rescue me from the wicked by your sword.

O LORD, by your hand save me from such men,
   from men of this world whose reward is in this life.

You still the hunger of those you cherish;
   their sons have plenty,
   and they store up wealth for their children.
And I—in righteousness I will see your face;
   when I awake, I will be satisfied with seeing
      your likeness. (Psalm 17:13-15)

As we seek to nurture the virtuous hunger for justice in our community, we are committed to ruthlessly examining every craving that runs contrary to Christ's. And while we are often dragging them (and ourselves) kicking and screaming to the cross, we clumsily continue to do so out of a deep and abiding hope that those selfish and empty pursuits of our hearts will be put to death. In their place a new hunger and thirst will grow—a hunger and thirst for a world where our relationships are characterized by humility, grace, generosity, mercy, peace and hope. As we've built friendships with those in our neighborhood, entering into their lives and homes, we've seen the shocking conditions that their landlords allow them to live in. Suddenly, concepts like tenant rights and affordable, dignified housing transform from ethical convictions into passionate and personal campaigns for justice and change.

The commitments we make to the poor—to our neighbors—whatever they may be, are not reflections of some noble gestures of holiness and self-sacrifice, but rather declarations of our satisfaction with Christ's kingdom as it breaks forth into our lives and the lives of those around us. And the thing about hunger and thirst is that, as soon as it is satisfied, it begins to build once again. Until his kingdom comes in its fullness, we must daily nurture this hunger for righteousness in our hearts and communities.

BLESSED ARE THE MERCIFUL,
FOR THEY WILL RECEIVE MERCY

Before his life was transformed by Christ, Francis was already showing signs of his godly character. One day while selling cloth to a local man, he was interrupted by a beggar seeking alms. Impatient with the beggar for not waiting until he was finished, Francis rebuked him and sent him away. It is doubtful that the beggar gave much thought to the matter, as being publicly despised and rejected was to be expected in his "line of work." However, Francis was overwhelmed with a sense of conviction regarding his cavalier dismissal of the poor man. Immediately he left in search of the beggar to whom he not only gave a generous gift but from whom he also begged forgiveness.

Even before the full flowering of his conversion, Francis knew better than to see acts of charity as though they were noble deeds of self-sacrifice. Instead he knew that the compassion and mercy he extended with each gift to the poor was but a small token of the undeserved compassion and mercy he had received from Christ in the forgiveness of his own sins and the provision of his needs. He recognized that in the eyes of God, he was no different than the beggar—no more important, no more deserving. In fact, in the moment he rudely dismissed the man, he proved himself far more destitute. While he had yet to fully understand it, his charity was not an act of personal sacrifice that proved his holiness but rather an acknowledgment that all that he had was already God's and he was just a humble servant entrusted with its care. This story gives us the first glimpse of Francis's deep sense of fraternity or mutuality, a guiding conviction that shaped the rest of his life and ministry.

It is only natural that—having led us from our total spiritual emptiness into the mourning contrition for our sinfulness, where our submitted humility to Christ gives birth to an insatiable hunger for justice—the Beatitudes should begin to concern themselves more and more with our relationship to others. In fact, the remainder of the Sermon on the Mount reflects this same direction and process. After all, it is only through loving God with our whole being that we are able, by his grace, to truly love others. And here we are reminded that in showing mercy we will be shown mercy ourselves.

Blessed are the merciful,
> for they will be shown mercy. (Matthew 5:7)

While mercy and grace are not to be confused, neither should they be considered entirely disconnected from each other. Grace is the unmerited gift of God to forgive us of our sins. Mercy is the compassionate response to the suffering that sin has caused. When we are merciful, it is only because we have received grace, for apart from grace, mercy is empty and without hope, a futile attempt to sweep back the ocean's tide with only a broom. This is critical to understand, for like Francis, when we live in mercy and compassion, when we make choices to show mercy and generosity to others, it points to the hope found in God's grace. It is not about us but about Christ.

Following as it does after the admonition to hunger for justice, this beatitude also makes clear that doing justice has more to do with caring for the suffering than it does confronting the sources of injustice. Both are important and without question mandated in Scripture as the responsibility of God's people. Yet Jesus is clearly placing an emphasis on mercy in respect to justice, bringing to mind the powerful prophetic mandate found in Micah 6:8, to "act justly and to love mercy and to walk humbly with your God." Why would he make that distinction? Is Jesus downplaying the need for the prophetic confrontation of injustice?

Having lived in my inner-city neighborhood for as long as I have, I am very aware of the systemic injustices that are ever present on our streets. Therefore, it is also a community that knows its fair share of activists. Most of these activists are well-intentioned, passionate people for whom I have the greatest respect. However, in talking to the more seasoned and mature among them, I have heard a common refrain: The danger of long-term activism can too often result in defining life by the brokenness of the world, by what the activist is against. Many of them say they struggle with dark thoughts and cynicism. Some secretly wonder if any good will come of their hard work of activism.

I believe that direct confrontation with systems of injustice is important, with activism playing a part.[3] The role of the prophetic voice has always been critical in confronting God's people and the wider society with their compromise and corruption, calling them to active, reparative repentance. Yet those voices are generally few. The Old Testament made the role of the prophet one to be taken very seriously and cautiously, with execution being a common consequence of misuse or abuse. It was often a lonely and thankless vocation.

While never denying the need for such prophetic voices, Jesus places an emphasis on expressions of justice that worked themselves out in active compassion and mercy to those in need. In James 4:17 we are reminded, "Anyone, then, who knows the good he ought to do and doesn't do it, sins." In the same way, the greatest weapons against injustice are acts of justice, mercy and compassion. It is not enough to know what is good and right and just; we must also act accordingly. Nor is it enough to simply be against that which is bad and wrong and unjust. As important as it is to confront injustice, our primary means of defeating it is by actively living in the opposite spirit of those who seek to destroy.

Further, by recognizing we are as much in need of mercy (and grace) as those we extend mercy to, we subvert the tendency we all have for coming to the rescue as the saviors of the lost and needy. We have one Savior, on whom we all absolutely and equally depend. This point was made beautifully in a story I heard from my wife's homeland, Australia. In response to some critical concerns facing an Aboriginal community in Queensland, the government sent a group of social workers and professionals to assess and respond to the problems. However, when they arrived, they were met at the entrance to the community by a group of local people, among them artist and activist Lilla Watson. The story goes that on behalf of her community Watson stepped forward and made the following statement: "If you have come here to help me, you are wasting your time. But if you have come because your liberation is bound up with mine, then let us work together."

In a culture that can make heroes out of people who champion the cause of the poor, we must remember that this truth about our mutuality of brokenness is critical. The temptation to take God's glory for ourselves is as old as the Garden of Eden. One way of discovering the seeds of this temptation in our heart is to examine who we are and are not willing to extend mercy to. While my neighborhood is largely filled with wonderful, hardworking people, there is also a very present and visible minority who are known and feared and even despised by many. Drug dealers, pimps, gang members and prostitutes are not abstract concepts or Hollywood characters on my block. They are my neighbors. Do I truly believe that I deserve mercy and grace no more than they do?

When we first moved into the community house we now call home, I remember getting up early one morning and standing on the back deck to take in the sunrise. As I turned to my left, I noticed a very pregnant teenage girl, probably no older than fourteen, nervously approaching my neighbor's back door. The house she was approaching was a known crack house, so there was little doubt about why she was there. I stood by in stunned disbelief as I listened to the girl desperately bargain for a hit, offering her body instead of the money she did not have. The arrangement was made and the girl disappeared into the dark doorway. Half an hour later, she stumbled out high as a kite, her shirt unbuttoned and her skirt falling from a naked hip.

In that moment my heart was filled with a burning anger toward the dealers in that house. I wanted to call down lightning from heaven to level the building where these so-called men would have sex with a pregnant kid in exchange for giving her a drug that was clearly destroying her and all too likely killing her unborn child. Even now, years later, I struggle with my anger toward that young girl who through casual irresponsibility was able to conceive a child—something my wife and I have not yet been able to accomplish—then treat herself and that child with reckless and destructive abandon. And this is just one story of hundreds that I have seen played out day after day in one community among countless others worldwide where such things happen. I honestly admit that grace is not my first impulse when thinking of these realities.

And yet to foreshadow what Jesus will further teach us later in the Sermon on the Mount, there are no degrees of sin in which one is measured as more acceptable than others. My lustful thoughts, then, are as detestable as those drug dealers' sexual exploitation of a damaged young girl. My hatred of her for her negligent treatment of an unborn child is as detestable as any of her actions that might lead to its death. Jesus' later contention that all sin is detestable and destructive has bearing on his assertion here that mercy characterizes the people of God. If we can get past the intellectual acknowledgment of this truth to the stark reality of it, we will truly know what it means to have our spirit broken, to mourn our wickedness, to be reduced to humble obedience and long for the righteousness and justice of God. Only then might we be able to truly understand that the mercy we extend to others is given regardless of their merit, because the grace and mercy we receive is equally undeserved. So the pregnant, fourteen-year-old drug addict, the drug-dealing thugs and me: none can be accused of being the "most lost"—no more than any of us can be congratulated as being the "least lost."

Finally, as Little Flowers Community has sought to extend mercy out of our own brokenness, we have also come to realize a difficult truth. The mercy we are promised in this beatitude comes from God. This is not a promise that as we are merciful to others, they will be merciful to us. Without question, as we are merciful to each other, it is not uncommon that we are extended mercy in return. However, this is neither a guarantee nor a right we can expect. While God can say to us, "Unless you forgive, you will not be forgiven," we can make no such demands of each other or of our neighbors. If we offer grace and mercy with any expectation for a "return on our investment," even if only sub-consciously, we have again fallen into the lie that we somehow deserve what we have received. Mercy is not always pragmatic, but it is always right.

BLESSED ARE THE PURE IN HEART, FOR THEY WILL SEE GOD

Jesus continued with the Beatitudes, saying:

> Blessed are the pure in heart,
>   for they will see God. (Matthew 5:8)

It is only when we recognize that every blessing from God—every expression of comfort and mercy—is extended to us as completely undeserved grace that we can understand what it means to be pure in heart. It is with that understanding that we see the hypocrisy of the Pharisees who claim purity as a result of their faithfulness and obedience to the law rather than the completely unmerited, undeserved gift of mercy that it is. For only God can make us pure of heart. What, then, does that mean? Jesus' words "Blessed are the pure in heart" don't make most people immediately think of the Wizard of Oz. However, there is a profound lesson to be learned from the story in this respect.

The Wizard of Oz is one of my childhood favorites. In it, Dorothy and her little dog Toto find themselves in a strange, unknown land. Dorothy soon learns that her only hope of getting home is to travel to the Emerald City for an audience with the great and powerful Wizard of Oz. On the way she is joined by three companions: Scarecrow, who has no brain; Tin Man, who has no heart; and Cowardly Lion, who has no courage. Each is assured by Dorothy that they will be given their brain, heart and courage (respectively) by the wonderful Wizard of Oz. And so they join hands and begin their journey.

After a series of adventures and mishaps, the little band of travelers are able to defeat the wicked witch, returning to the wizard for their promised rewards. However, when they discover that he is a fraud—no wizard at all!—they are outraged, especially Scarecrow, Tin Man and Lion. However, the wizard assures them that they've already had everything they're seeking; they just needed to prove it to themselves. Dorothy too learns that her own way home has always been available to her, but she needed to learn that she's always had what she was looking for at home.

Upon closer inspection we see that each of Dorothy's companions lack something critical to every person: a mind (Scarecrow), emotions (Tin Man) and the will or courage to act (Lion). Interestingly, the Jewish people understood the heart to be the indivisible realm of their mind, their emotions and their will. In many ways Dorothy's companions were aspects of her own heart, divided and uncertain. It was only when they united under a singular purpose that they proved themselves whole and reached their destination. It is this singular devotion of mind, emotions and will that Jesus is referring to when he speaks of the pure in heart.

While the concept of purity of heart was by no means new to Jesus' Jewish listeners, his emphasis on this inner purity over and above the external purity (reflected in the rituals and rites of Judaism) was not one of exclusion but of emphasis. After all, when the inner dynamics of our mind, emotions and will come together, they inevitably produce external behavior. However, Jesus was pointing to the internal character, not the external actions themselves, as the place of necessary purity. In other words, our deeds do not make us pure, but our purity (which is by God's grace alone) makes our actions righteous.

And like the tale of Dorothy and her companions, our heart (mind, emotions and will) is pure only when it is submitted and obedient to God alone. After all, purity suggests a singularity of substance, where in refining silver, even a speck of previous gold would be considered an impurity. Impurity of the heart, then, can be anything good or bad that distracts us from absolute obedience to Christ. He is not interested in our righteous works, even if they rival those of Mother Teresa herself, if they are not born out of a pure heart.

All too often the subtle, "justifiable" compromises of our hearts make them impure. While blatant acts of evil will obviously sully the heart, so too will acts of noble goodness if they run contrary to the will of God. While greed is obvious to most of us, we might miss the subtle danger of compromising our call to radical obedience to Christ in the name of "good stewardship." Few would argue with the sins of indulging sexual lust, but we might gloss over compromising our calling in hope of finding Mr. or Mrs. Right. And though we would reject the pursuit of power for its own sake, we might miss the true power of a calling to a life of service, convinced that we can do more good from a position of worldly authority. In the end, the measure of our purity is the active loyalty in our hearts and lives to Christ. We must daily ask ourselves: *Where in my heart has something other than Christ taken first place?*

When we pursue this purity of heart, we are given the hope that we will indeed see God! After all, if we are single-minded in our devotion to God, he will be all we see in our daily lives. His love, his truth, his hope, his peace—all will become clear to us in the world around us. His words will come alive in our hearts. His Spirit will quicken us to life and purpose. When we are pure in heart, we will see God precisely because he is all we will want to see. This is not a pie-in-the-sky, sentimental expectation, but rather it is a very real transformation of the heart—mind, will and emotions—that opens our eyes to see beyond our circumstances to the unconquerable hope and love of God.

Further, as the pattern of the Beatitudes leads us to broken and humbled lives of justice and mercy, we will see God because this single-minded devotion will bring us daily into the presence of others who are created in God's image. Even in the brokenness of those on the margins, Jesus promises that our loving service to them is service directly to him (Matthew 25:40)! Francis powerfully demonstrated this truth in an encounter with someone least likely to be associated with the image of God: a leper.

While most people of Francis's day feared leprosy not only for the death sentence it ultimately brings but also because of the fears and superstitions attached to the illness, Francis was especially terrified. He was known to have fled from the sounds of the lepers' bells, which they rang to warn others of their coming. God, though, was at work in Francis's heart, preparing him for his true conversion. One day, while riding outside of Assisi, Francis came upon a leper, raising fear and horror within him. However, he overcame his impulse and approached the man. Giving the leper a coin, Francis took his diseased hand and kissed it. Though it was a difficult act of self-discipline, he was able to kiss the leper because growing inside him was the uncontainable impulse of a devoted follower of Christ coming face to face with his beloved Master.[4]

Dorothy Day, writer, social activist and cofounder of the Catholic Worker Movement, has long been an inspiration of mine in this respect. I first came to learn about Day when, on a whim, I rented a copy of the movie *Entertaining Angels: The Dorothy Day Story*. Near the end of the film Day has become discouraged by the constant demands and thankless work of serving the poorest of the poor in Depression-era New York City. As a storm shatters the night sky with streaks of lightning, Day wanders into a large, empty church, and walks toward the crucifix at the front. Tears of exhaustion and anger roll down her face as she confronts Jesus:

> Where are you? Why won't you answer me? I need you! These brothers and sisters of Yours, the ones You want me to love—let me tell You something. They smell. They have lice and tuberculosis. Am I to find You in them? Well, You're ugly. You drink and You wet Your pants and You vomit. How can anyone ever love You?[5]

This encounter is reflective of the soul of this humble woman who struggled to remain pure of heart as she served God and others. In this powerful scene her idealism of seeing and encountering Christ in the poor collided with reality. We must never forget that as long as sin and suffering remain, we will find Christ among the broken and the lost. We must never idealize or romanticize the nature of the lifestyle this calls us to, nor the people whom it calls us to love. We must go in with our eyes open to the messy and costly reality of love. In the face of this cost we realize that only with a pure heart can we hope to persevere and truly see the face of God in the other.

In addition to calling us to sacrificial service, this truth also places an unforgiving mirror before our own brokenness. Here again we are reminded that we are no different, no better than those we deem the "most lost." In the light of Christ our need for grace is no less absolute. And yet the beauty of this truth is also that just as we find Christ through loving and serving others, so too can others come to see Christ in our brokenness. For while sin marred the image of God we bear, we are being transformed into the image of Christ through the work of the cross. And just as the cross brings us together in our shared need for forgiveness, so too is that very unity reflecting the resurrected Lord who saved us before a waiting and watching world.

One of the most powerful expressions of Jesus' demonstration of this purity of heart is found in Matthew 21 after his triumphal entry into Jerusalem. After cleansing the temple of the money-lenders, many of the blind and the lame come to him in the temple and are healed. What is often missed by readers today is that Jesus was going against a deeply embedded tradition laid out in the Old Testament. David forbade the blind and the lame from entering the temple (2 Samuel 5:8), and the priestly rules forbade them from making sacrifices (Leviticus 21:17). To enter the temple for sacrifice, one had to be without defect, because defects would dese-crate the sanctuary.

With the arrival of Jesus as the true high priest, the last, best and only sacrifice, the tables are suddenly turned. Instead of wholeness being a prerequisite for entering into the presence of God, it is in the very act of entering into the presence of Christ— following him into holiness—that the blind and lame are made whole! The categories are reversed. The expected commerce, typi-cal to the temple, is driven out, and those who are ritually unclean are welcomed, defying the typical expectations of moral and spir-itual categories. Therefore, as we extend the mercy of Christ to others, we are to welcome them alongside ourselves, in our bro-kenness, to find forgiveness and wholeness in his presence. How different is this from the demands we so often place on people before they enter into our communities of faith?

This freedom to approach the presence of God together in the midst of our brokenness has been liberating for many of us in Little Flowers Community. Being part of a church where we do not have to achieve a certain level of perfection to be welcomed or put on a false piety to hide our sin is freeing. It is by no means a license for us to remain satisfied in mediocrity and sin. Rather, like Jesus dying for us while we were yet unrepentant, ungrateful sinners, it is the true nature of love and grace extended to all.

Blessed Are the Peacemakers
and the Persecuted

Matthew 5:9-12

While Canadian cities enjoy relatively less gun violence than many other cities around the world, Canadians do not have to be familiar with the sound of a gunshot to recognize what it is. My wife and I froze in our seats in the living room one afternoon as the sound of gunshots broke the silence of an otherwise pleasant, sunny day. Not only was it obviously the sound of a firearm, but it had clearly been fired rather close to our home. After waiting for a few moments to make sure the shots had ceased, I threw on my sandals and headed to the door.

Sure enough, just over a hundred feet from our front door I saw a young man lying on the ground, clutching his bleeding leg. A few people on the scene held cell phones to their ears and the sound of sirens assured me that the ambulance (and police) were on their way. As the paramedics loaded the young man into the back of the ambulance, he turned his head, and with a start I realized that I knew him. He was an African immigrant, the friend of one of my coworkers, whom I had met several times. While he had previously been involved in a local gang, he had since gotten out of that lifestyle. However, old gang grudges die hard. Thankfully his injuries were not serious and he recovered fully over the summer.

While violence in the neighborhood was nothing new (I had witnessed all kinds of assault and abuse from the vantage point of my own front yard), this was the first time such extreme violence had occurred to someone I knew. It tore the issues of gang violence out of the abstract and deeply humanized it for me, and in so doing it created an urgency in me to do something. But what could we do? How could we respond to such widespread violence with any hope of making a difference?

> Blessed are the peacemakers,
>> for they will be called sons of God. (Matthew 5:9)

At the time of the shooting, though "blessed are the peacemakers" sounded nice, I was at a loss for what it meant.

Undoubtedly, the people who heard Jesus' words that day had many of the same questions, but for far more pressing issues. Under the ruthless military rule of Rome, many of the Jews began to wonder how God would liberate them from so powerful an enemy. Some groups, like the Zealots, believed that they were to rise up in arms against this superior force and, like David defeating Goliath, demonstrate God's favor by driving the Romans out of Israel forever. Many Jews, while perhaps not willing to join the ranks of the Zealots, sympathized with their cause. So when Jesus said "Blessed are the peacemakers," it seemed that he was rejecting such an option. Jesus was pointing to the fulfillment of his kingdom that would not come through violence but through an active, intentional pursuit of peace.

I have since come to realize that peace is far more than the absence of violence, just as goodness is so much more than the absence of evil. When Jesus spoke of peace, he was referring to an all-encompassing state of health, harmony and justice that even extended to his enemies. Images of the lion and lamb lying together powerfully capture the seemingly ridiculous, unnatural peace he is calling us to. By peace, Jesus is referring to something better known as *shalom*. *Shalom* is a Hebrew word that in this context means far more than the absence of violence or even an established truce between enemies. Rather, central to its meaning is the concept of wholeness, one that includes the individual but extends also to broader society and even the world. John Driver explains:

> It meant well-being, or health, or salvation in its fullest sense, material as well as spiritual. It described the situation of well-being which resulted from authentically whole (healed) relationships among people, as well as between persons and God. According to the Old Testament prophets, shalom reigned in Israel when there was social justice, when the cause of the poor and the weak was vindicated, when there was equal opportunity for all, in short, when the people enjoyed salvation according to the intention of God expressed in his covenant.[1]

We are called to make *this* kind of peace. Reminiscent of Micah 6:8, where we are called to *do* justice, here Jesus is telling us that we are to *create* shalom. However, understanding this, we are now faced with a monumental challenge. How do we create such universal, all-encompassing peace?

First, we must realize what has brought us to this point in the Beatitudes. While not a formula to follow or so many easy steps to achieve world peace, the pattern of the Beatitudes points us toward virtuous lives, shaped by Christ, which go a long way to producing shalom in our hearts and in our communities. Second, it is not up to us to finally and for all time achieve shalom, only to be makers of shalom, creators of peace in our lives and our immediate contexts. Christ alone can inaugurate true shalom, and it is only through him that any of our efforts have any meaning or hope.

That being said, Jesus puts to rest the notion that his people are called to only (or even primarily) the spiritual needs of the world, to "save souls." Shalom destroys the false dichotomy between the so-called social gospel and spiritual gospel, leaving instead the fullness of God's truly good news for all of creation. An emphasis on either end of the spectrum that excludes or minimizes the other misses the heart of the true gospel. We must resist the temptation to reduce or simplify the gospel in order to make it more accessible or acceptable; we must seek to embrace it in its fullness. And this means a lot of work, sacrifice and perseverance in a world where a very real enemy will push back with ruthless force. Being a peacemaker is all too often a thankless, even hated, vocation. It forces us to be about the work of reconciliation at all costs.

This chapter (and this book) does not leave enough room to explore this critical concept of peacemaking in more detail. For Little Flowers Community it means, in part, that we are a peace church. That is, we are a community of Christians that believes nonviolent resistance, rather than so-called redemptive violence, is central to Christ's calling to us to be peacemakers. How this works itself out is not always clear or easy, but the question of violence in our world and the church's response to (and participation in) it—both in the private and social spheres of life—is critical for us to address. All too often the church has been complicit in the use of violence. In our neighborhood, where violence is all too common, we cannot afford that complicity.

Many sincere and responsible followers of Christ make room for occasions of "redemptive violence," even when it can only be thought of as a last resort.[2] However, we believe that Christ calls us to abhor and grieve violence in every form. Peace must be our first, best and only option in the face of violence, brokenness and sin. Should a Christian believe that violence can be used justly in certain circumstances, I can only hope that any such situation would be arrived at with great lament and mourning and only as a last resort. For regardless of our theological position, violence should be abhorrent and painfully upsetting for every Christian. For Little Flowers Community it means choosing to remain within the violence, confronting it with the weapons of love and grace, even when it does not "work." Again, Jesus' commands are not always pragmatic, but they are always right.

While St. Francis was not a pacifist by today's standards, we cannot deny that his example planted the seeds for the modern Franciscan peace ethic, known and proven around the world by women and men who have laid down their lives for God's peaceful kingdom. Just as the humility and meekness of Francis gave birth to the Franciscan tradition of peacemaking, so too is our own conviction of being peacemakers born out of the purity of heart that comes through Christ alone.

FOR THEY WILL BE CALLED CHILDREN OF GOD

When Jesus said that the peacemakers would be blessed and called the "sons of God," it might have struck the Jews as a rather odd thing for him to say. After all, they were already God's chosen people, his children, the famed children of Israel. Yet it would not have taken them long to realize that Jesus was intentionally linking their identity as God's people with the task of working to bring shalom into the world. By doing this Jesus reminded his listeners that their covenant with God was clear—they were only blessed so that they could be a blessing to all nations. Their identity as the children of God was contingent on their obedience to the promises they made to God.

We make this mistake all too often ourselves as Christians. We present the gospel as the free gift of salvation available to all, yet we often fail to include (both in evangelism and discipleship) the equal truth that the means of this salvation is the absolute surrender of our entire lives to our Lord and Master. We can only be saved through his death on the cross, being raised with him as his body. Therefore, as his body, we must be wholly about his purposes. When we proudly bear the name of Christ—calling ourselves Christians—but then put him second (or worse) in any aspect of our lives, we blaspheme his name. This is what it truly means to use the Lord's name in vain.

But God does not call us to be merely his slaves, though he is indeed our Lord and Master. Rather, he calls us his children, extending to us an identity like no other. To be called his family, his children, is a grace beyond all comprehension. Our commitment to build with him this kingdom of shalom is not the forced labor of a slave but the apprenticed work of children learning the family trade. Jesus masterfully reminds us of our very real obligations to God while framing it in a way that affirms the immense blessedness of being part of such a kingdom. Blessed *are* the peacemakers!

For a church with so many young adults, there is a surprising number of people at Little Flowers Community who have lost one or both of their parents. Whether through death, estrangement, mental illness or some other loss, the longing for a true parental love runs deep in their hearts. In the midst of our brokenness we have the promise that God not only loves us but invites us to participate in his great work as his apprenticed and beloved children. That he chooses to work in, through and with us for his glory is a life-transforming affirmation that in itself plants the seeds of shalom in each of our hearts. Few things better motivate us to build shalom in our lives, our community and our world than this fatherly blessing.

BLESSED ARE THOSE PERSECUTED FOR RIGHTEOUSNESS BECAUSE OF CHRIST

When I was still a teenager, I had the opportunity to meet a group of people from different parts of the world; each shared their life story and their faith journey. It was one of the first times I had encountered such a diverse group of Christians, and I was held rapt by each person's tale. However, there is one story that remains with me more than any other. A young woman from an Eastern European communist nation shared what it was like for her to be a Christian in her country when she was a child.

Being part of a Christian home in her country was a great risk. Even socially, children of Christian parents faced great persecution, ridicule and threats. While at school, she was once brought in front of the whole class by her teacher, who began to denigrate Christianity and all Christians. Her teacher then cruelly demanded that she reject Christ before the whole class. She froze in fear, but said nothing. The other students watched with fascination, some with cruel expectation. Again her teacher demanded that she reject Christ, and again she remained silent. However, when her teacher threatened to have her parents arrested and thrown in prison, this poor young girl burst into tears and desperately denied Christ. She carried the guilt and shame of that moment with her well into her adult years.

This woman's story left a significant impression on me. Up until that moment, persecution for one's faith had been purely academic to me. At best I had heard stories of brave Christians, but I had never met one personally, never called one friend. And then here this woman was, second-guessing her faith as a result of a tragic childhood experience. I was humbled, even ashamed at how flippantly I had treated my faith in light of the great freedom I had to practice it. To this day her story comes to mind whenever I feel I am being treated unfairly because of following Christ. Clearly, I have never experienced genuine persecution for Christ.

The final beatitude is, in fact, two beatitudes. Or rather, it is the only beatitude on which Jesus places a double emphasis. As the capstone of the blessings, it is not surprising that he brings special attention to them:

Blessed are those who are persecuted because of
   righteousness,
   for theirs is the kingdom of heaven.

Blessed are you when people insult you, persecute you
and falsely say all kinds of evil against you because of me.
Rejoice and be glad, because great is your reward in heaven,
for in the same way they persecuted the prophets who were
before you. (Matthew 5:10-12)

Here we are told that the righteousness/justice that we are hun-
gering and thirsting after—the justice that is at the heart of the
peace/shalom we are called to create—will likely bring us persecution and suffering. Our overfamiliarity with this Scripture
might cause us to miss how absolutely ridiculous this statement
would have sounded to Jesus' followers. It is a *blessing* to be persecuted? The people were familiar with the righteousness of the
Pharisees, whose dedicated adherence to the external requirements of the law made them men of authority to be respected and
admired. The righteousness Jesus was requiring would bring suffering, maybe even death. Talk about a flawed sales pitch!

Jesus goes on to promise that those who suffer for working for
justice and peace will receive the kingdom of heaven. He was not
offering some future, eternal reward after death (though that is
also implicit in his words). Rather, he intentionally used the present tense to say that the promised kingdom, the fulfillment of the
covenant promises of God, was immediately available, if only in
part, to those who suffered for the sake of his righteousness. This
is what it was all about! Jesus was offering the very thing they had
been longing for, here and now, as long as they were willing to be
faithful to God's calling (as seen through the previous beatitudes),
even if it brought them suffering and cost them everything.

Jesus does not stop here but goes on to restate the blessing even
more clearly, shifting from third person to second, making it even

more personal and immediate to his listeners. Here Jesus shows his hand, linking faithful obedience to God with faithful obedience to himself. He promises that anyone who suffers for *his* sake is blessed. Suddenly all the previous beatitudes are understood through the lens of faithfulness to Christ, which is synonymous with faithfulness to God.

Consider, for example, the blessing for the peacemakers, who will be called children of God. Here Jesus is linking the name of God with his own name, planting the seed for our future identity as Christians. This is proven in 1 Peter 4:12-19, where this beatitude is so clearly reiterated to the early Christian community. Specifically, we see in verse 16, "However, if you suffer as a Christian, do not be ashamed, but praise God that you bear that name." The name *Christian* (and thus Christ) is clearly equated with our identity as children of God, with verse 17 going on to call Christ's followers the "family of God." So in the Sermon on the Mount Jesus is making his first and clearest demand for our loyalty to him, not merely as a rabbi or prophet, but as someone equal to God himself.

Why would we be persecuted? Why should our faithful commitment to build a kingdom characterized by humility, mercy, peace, reconciliation and justice cause people to hate us and harm us? The sad truth is this: injustice is a profitable venture. I am not talking about Dr. Evil laughing maniacally as he plots how to steal one gazillion dollars from the world (pinky raised to corner of his mouth). That kind of caricature of injustice is rarely accurate and never helpful. Instead, we must realize that the power structures of the world, be they political, economic, military or even religious, have a long history of establishing their power base through the casual neglect or blatant exploitation of others (all too often, the poor). To a large degree the Western economy, for example, has been built and sustained by exploiting poorer nations who are willing to compromise basic human rights and dignities, and sacrifice their natural resources, in the hope of economic gain. As we become a people characterized by making justice in the world, calling others to join us, we actively threaten those very systems and powers of injustice.

This is why Jesus compares such faithful followers to the prophets. As mentioned earlier, a primary role of a prophet was to confront injustice in the midst of God's people and the broader society. Throughout the Old Testament the prophets return again and again to the themes of faithfulness to God's laws and just treatment of the poor and the marginalized. Our persecution for Christ is linked to our active resistance to injustice. This undermines the idea that God calls his people to minister only to the "spiritual" (nonmaterial) needs of the world. He makes no such distinction, and neither should we.

That Jesus calls us to rejoice and be glad in the midst of suffering makes two powerful statements. First, he reminds us that our joy is found in his blessings and promises, not in our circumstances. St. Francis remained so joyful in the midst of his difficult life that many called him a fool for Christ, a title he very much liked. Second, it says just as much about how we are *not* to respond. Our impulse to violently and vehemently defend against and counterattack those who persecute us is only natural, but Jesus refuses us that option. He knows that shalom cannot be built at the end of a sword. His kingdom is not like the kingdoms of the world.

At Little Flowers we are very careful not to throw around the word *persecution*. At one time or another all of us have wondered if our lack of persecution was somehow an indictment that we were not living as Christ commanded, and perhaps there is some truth to that. However, in the light of the freedom and peace we do experience as Western Christians, we need to be aware of two potential dangers in this respect. First, we must be careful not to overinflate our struggles as though they are persecution when they clearly are not. While we can argue about the challenges faced in a culture where prayer is no longer permitted in public schools, I believe it dishonors the prophets and martyrs who have gone before us (and who truly suffer even now around the world) to claim that we are persecuted and suffering for such things. This is what I call becoming "paper-cut martyrs," people who inflate their own righteousness by making it seem as if facing legitimate but relatively minor struggles and challenges is like standing before lions in an arena. Let us not dishonor God or those who truly suffer in any attempt to boost our own spiritual status. After all, it is for *Christ's* sake that we suffer; it's no reflection of our own merit or worth.

Second, if we make mistakes or treat people poorly in the name of God, it is not persecution when they attack us or Christianity as a result. It is shameful, for example, to claim that we are being persecuted by the "homosexual community" when they lash out against the church. The fact is that Western Christians have little idea what it has been like for the millions of gay, lesbian, bisexual and transgendered people to live with such universal hatred and abuse, often at the hands of the church. That Christians have largely mistreated these people for centuries is not even debatable. While hatred is never justified, it is not difficult to understand why we have been cast as the enemy. We have earned their distrust and revilement through our choices. Therefore, to call their attacks persecution is like willfully knocking down a hornet's nest and then claiming innocence when getting stung.

Francis was far more aware of the price of following Jesus. In fact, when he found himself before the sultan during the crusades, he might well have expected, even longed for, martyrdom. He understood that the very word *martyr* had its roots in the Greek that means "witness." In other words, he understood and was willing to face suffering and death—not for their own sake but as the result of being a witness to Christ by living and proclaiming his good news. While martyrdom was sometimes exploited in the church, people in medieval times were seemingly far more willing than we are to give their lives if it meant pleasing the God of salvation. Apart from the unhealthy transactional mentality that often accompanied such devotion, we would do well to consider why our willingness pales in comparison to so many faithful Christians who have come before us (and the many throughout the world today).

These final beatitudes foreshadow the inevitable suffering and death that come with being a Christian, for they point clearly to the cross of Christ. The undeniable sin and brokenness in the world, in our communities and in our hearts mean that suffering and death are inevitable, even necessary. However, we are blessed! We can rejoice and be glad because not even death can stop the kingdom that is breaking forth. In fact, it is through death that the miracle of resurrection brings hope and salvation to all creation. As we continue through the Sermon on the Mount, we must always read it in the brilliant light of the Beatitudes, for they are the key to understanding the rest of Christ's message.

Of Salt, Light and the Law

Matthew 5:13-32

The final beatitude Jesus shares changes everything. Unlike the previous beatitudes, in Matthew 5:11-12 Jesus addresses his listeners directly. Where before he proclaimed "Blessed are the . . . ," here he reiterates his final point, but this time pointedly declares, "Blessed are *you* . . ." Both this personal address and the lengthened nature of the beatitude force us to recognize its special significance. And Jesus is not subtle with the difference, for this time he places faithfulness to himself as central to this blessing. Where the previous blessings could be understood through the Old Testament (even if challenging the status-quo understanding of those texts), by placing himself at the heart of the climactic blessing, Jesus declares himself the only way through which any of the blessings are possible. This radical claim hooked his listeners instantly. If he claimed to be the crux in us becoming the people of the Beatitudes, then surely what followed would clarify what that would mean. And the remaining Sermon does just that.

SALT OF THE EARTH

While I now live in the heart of an urban community, I grew up outside the small, picturesque, rural community of Rainy River.

Hunting and fishing were not only popular tourist attractions for the area but a way of life for most of the locals. Our own house was built on the banks of the wide river, where we could cast our lines out to catch dinner. My father was also a hunter, killing his first moose with a bow and arrow. That huge animal filled our freezer for many months. I grew up often hearing stories of hunting adventures, of taking down a raging black bear or a twelve-point buck from an impossible distance. And while it's rarely practiced anymore, I also heard various techniques for curing meat—most popularly, when refrigeration was not available, using salt to preserve it for long periods of time. Essentially, salting the meat inhibits the growth of microorganisms and bacteria as it draws out the moisture, thus allowing it to be preserved far longer. It is a bit of an acquired taste to the uninitiated, but it works rather well.

This is one of the reasons why salt was so valuable to the people of Jesus' day, where a deep freeze was most certainly not available. Salt was so important to protecting and preserving food sources that it was not uncommon for Roman soldiers to be paid their salary in salt. For this very reason, both the words *soldier* and *salary* find their root in the word *salt*. Salt remains a significantly valuable and important commodity even today. For most of us in the Western world, salt is a common seasoning we enjoy (remembering to do so in moderation for our health, of course). Because of this, we might miss the significance of Jesus' words when he call us the "salt of the earth."

> You are the salt of the earth. But if the salt loses its saltiness, how can it be made salty again? It is no longer good for anything, except to be thrown out and trampled by men. (Matthew 5:13)

With this powerful imagery, Jesus reveals what happens when the community of the Beatitudes comes into being in the world. Living as his virtuous people according to his kingdom rule, the

Christian community becomes an agent of preservation against the decay and rot of sin in the world. We literally halt the destructive forces of injustice, greed and lust! By becoming a living alternative, we subvert the powers of darkness by allowing the world a glimpse of a new and better way of life. In essence, through our redeemed brokenness and relentless faithfulness, the world will see Christ and the hope of true salvation.

This reality entails a difficult tension, for while the salt is essentially and actively present *in* the world, it still remains distinctly *other than* and *different from* the world, just as the salt and meat in the curing process—while integrated—represent two distinct parts. After all, the kingdom that is breaking through into the world in our lives and by his Spirit is by necessity something altogether new and different from what the world has known before. Here Jesus calls us to live in the difficult but necessary tension between isolation or withdrawal from the world, on the one hand, and the compromise of our identity, vocation and morality on the other. Withdrawal from the world means abandoning it to the decay of sin, while compromising means we are no different than the world, leaving us just as prone to sin's destructive decay. For the sake of God and the lost, we must struggle with this tension daily. How? By remaining the people of Christ described in the Beatitudes.

This dynamic deeply shaped the Franciscan order. While Francis unquestionably drew inspiration from the monastic Benedictines (without whom the Franciscan order might never have come into existence), he did not believe that God was calling him to a monastic life. The word *monk*, after all, comes from the Greek word *monachos*, which means "solitary" or "alone." In other words, monastics gathered together to step apart from the world for the purpose of prayer and worship. Francis valued the contemplative disciplines and the mutuality of community, but rather than a community removed from the world, Francis imagined a community sent into the world. So while Franciscans would live distinctly different lives around their vows and rule of life, they would do so in the world among the common people. They believed that their devotion to God in the midst of the people would be a sign of hope, salvation and preservation to a watching world.

There is no "preservation" in making public spectacles at funerals, hurling hateful epithets at gay people during gay pride parades or exploiting natural disasters as opportunities to rail against "biblical immorality." The curative process that Jesus alludes to here is intimate, personal. The salt gets to know the meat it cures. The challenge of this kind of preservation is extraordinarily difficult, facing the very real risks of both extremes. At Little Flowers this has meant wrestling with what it means for us to be a community that shamelessly acknowledges the reality and consequences of sin, yet can also be a place of hospitality and grace for sinners—not through some pretentious humility that says "But for the grace of God go I," but because we know our own very real and present brokenness and sin.

All too often, when we consider being "in the world, but not of the world," being entirely *other* and different than the world, we are tempted to consider ourselves better than the world. While we are called to be something new, Jesus does not allow for this arrogance. In fact, considering the analogy, Jesus clearly places us in a subservient position. The point of salting meat is to preserve the meat. The salt is essential and much valued, but saving the meat is the end; the salt is merely the means. Even then the salt provides only a delay in the decaying process. In the same way, Jesus is affirming that while the world is indeed corrupted by sin, it is his priority to preserve it, to extend hope and grace to it. Why? Because he loves all of creation so very much. How? Through his children, his church, his body. Ultimately, only he can reverse decay and death. While we are more than a mere means to an end for God, Jesus makes it very clear that, should we not remain "salty," we are of no use to him. Again, Jesus is linking our identity in him with his mission of redemption and shalom.

LIGHT OF THE WORLD

After calling us to be agents of preservation against decay and death in the world, Jesus goes on to call us the "light of the world."

> You are the light of the world. A city on a hill cannot be hidden. Neither do people light a lamp and put it under a bowl. Instead they put it on its stand, and it gives light to everyone in the house. In the same way, let your light shine before men, that they may see your good deeds and praise your Father in heaven. (Matthew 5:14-16)

Where before we were commanded to be actively present in the world, now he is making it further clear that our presence is to be explicitly visible in the world as well—visible through the light of our good works. Our faithfulness to good is evidenced by public acts of service, sacrifice and love, the very deeds, born of the Beatitudes, that give glory to God—that is, the spirit of poverty, contrition, humility, justice, mercy, submission, peacemaking, and even suffering for righteousness and Christ. These good deeds, rooted in our brokenness, give glory to God, his grace and his mercy and stand in stark contrast to the self-serving works done before others, which Jesus denounces later in Matthew 6:1 (see chap. 8).

That such righteousness can exist without being self-glorifying has been illustrated to me in a most unlikely way. Due to the high levels of addiction so common to the inner city, there also tend to be a large number of recovery programs in cities, especially twelve-step groups like Alcoholics Anonymous. At their best I find them to be communities who have chosen to openly acknowledge their brokenness, yet strive together to live a better alternative. In their refusal to deny their past and present failings, they are able to stand together and forge a common unity that transforms their brokenness into strength. Many of these diligent people are then able to go on, make amends for their mistakes, and build a better future for themselves and their families. In this way they acknowledge their "higher power" for their ultimate transformation without denying their own responsibility for past mistakes and present decisions. In the same way our own commitment to good deeds are not noble acts of self-sacrifice but the grateful devotion of broken people who against all hope find redemption and salvation in Jesus Christ, extending that promise to others. These good deeds are not characteristic of the especially devout, but represent the expected baseline and standard for all believers.

The fact is, we *are* his light, whether we let it be seen by the world or not. If our lives and works are not shaped by the Beatitudes—if we are not doing these good works in front of a watching world—then we are hiding his light, quenching it, keeping it from those he intends it for. Just as salt does not exist for its own sake but for the preservation of the meat, so too light is not the glowing halo of our own holiness but a beacon of life and hope to those lost in darkness. There is never a moment, even in the privacy of our own homes, where we cease to be that light. It is both far-reaching, like a city on a hill, and personal, like a lamp in a small room. And if our lives do not shine with the light of these good works, we rob the message of the gospel of its very authority. Again, we use the name of Christ in vain and prove ourselves unfaithful.

Whereas our role as salt of the earth is preservation against the decay and death of sin, our role as the light of the world is to give life and hope, like the sun giving life to thriving crops or a lighted window promising a warm homecoming. As the community of the Beatitudes we must represent both aspects of God's mission, without emphasizing one over the other. If we fight the dangers of sin in the world to the exclusion of bringing the light of life, we risk becoming legalists, being defined more by what we are not than by the God of grace and love. If we seek to be the light of life and hope but deny the very real and present dangers of sin, we expose ourselves and others to its very corruption, compromise and accommodation. With this synthesis of being both the salt and the light—bearers of morality and ministry, of righteousness and justice—the Law and the Prophets come together. It is here that God calls us to love him with all that we are and to love our neighbor as ourselves.

FULFILLING THE LAW AND THE PROPHETS

Many of us at Little Flowers grew up in the church, but not everyone found that to be a positive experience. While grateful that they came to know Christ through these communities, some were raised in contexts of abusive legalism. Having spent my entire life as an evangelical, I am all too aware of this tendency toward judgment over grace, of rules over freedom and of discipline over devotion (though I was blessed in that my childhood church largely modeled healthy evangelicalism). My point here is by no means to criticize certain segments of the church, for we are all one, and such criticisms must be addressed by all Christians as *our* problem, not *theirs*. However, I mention it because many young Christians are beginning to leave such traditions for expressions of Christianity where they find communities of genuine hospitality, celebration, mutuality and freedom. Where no such alternatives are found, many are looking outside the church altogether. As a community that has struggled to embrace the life Jesus called us to, Little Flowers has inevitably appealed to many such people.

However, we soon came to realize that as we fled one extreme, we faced the very real risk of running directly into the arms of another. For some, the liberty that came with being in a community where authenticity was both safe and encouraged, where an individual's acceptance was not primarily based on adherence to certain behavioral requirements or rules, was new and exciting. Once forbidden to drink any alcohol, they were now given the freedom to make their own responsible choices. However, not everyone was prepared to handle such freedom, and some plunged into all-too-frequent bouts of drunkenness. This same pattern presented itself in other areas as well, such as with boundaries in romantic relationships or with respect and propriety in worship. We soon recognized that such freedom placed us on a path between two dangerous extremes. Like the mythical beasts Scylla and Charybdis in Homer's *Odyssey* that threatened passing ships on either side, we needed to learn to navigate carefully and appropriately between these extremes.

When Jesus described the life of the Beatitudes, of a people whose identity reflected God precisely from within their suffering and persecution, the people would have found great hope. And when he went on to call them the salt of the earth and the light of the world, they would have been thrilled. After all, for so long the only models of righteousness they saw were the Pharisees and teachers of the law, who were characterized by rigorous adherence to the external demands of the law. They might have begun to suspect that Jesus was giving them an escape from the law, as though he was rejecting it as nothing more than legalistic fundamentalism. Like us at Little Flowers Community, they faced a freedom like none they had ever considered.

Jesus, however, did not allow such an assumption to take root.

Do not think that I have come to abolish the Law or the Prophets; I have not come to abolish them but to fulfill them. I tell you the truth, until heaven and earth disappear, not the smallest letter, not the least stroke of a pen, will by any means disappear from the Law until everything is accomplished. Anyone who breaks one of the least of these commandments and teaches others to do the same will be

called least in the kingdom of heaven, but whoever practices
and teaches these commands will be called great in the
kingdom of heaven. For I tell you that unless your righteousness surpasses that of the Pharisees and the teachers of
the law, you will certainly not enter the kingdom of heaven.
(Matthew 5:17-20)

The radical grace and mercy that Christ was presenting was not
a license for moral compromise or even a new law that abolished
the old. For the intention of both the Law and the Prophets was
exactly what Jesus was proclaiming, what he was doing and being.
The true intention of the law called us to be the preserving presence in a world of sin, and the prophets called for us to bring the
light of God's justice and shalom to everyone. In Christ both of
those ends are fulfilled, in part through us, his children, his community of the Beatitudes. He achieves those ends. As noted in
chapter one, the Gospel of Matthew often frames Jesus in the light
of Moses. Here, just as Moses led the Jews out of the bondage of
Egypt, both in its physical slavery and in its cultural and spiritual
colonialism, so too was Jesus leading Israel out of the bondage of
legalism and sin. Both times people were extended liberty from
captivity, but they were also, in both instances, called to radical
obedience and faithfulness to God. To use the liberty that Jesus
brings as a justification for mediocrity and compromise is offensive beyond words.

What Jesus was rejecting was the abuse, misuse and misrepre-
sentation of the Law and the Prophets. The Pharisees and the
teachers of the law adhered to the law only insofar as it was to
their own advantage. They sought to perform, to mimic the external expressions of lawfulness, but it was just that—mimicry, play-
acting, the very definition of hypocrisy, even when such adherence was motivated by a genuine desire to do right. The Law and
the Prophets called for a transformation of the heart that would

produce the external righteousness and justice they demanded. And only through Christ is such a fulfillment even possible. For, in the face of our own sin and sinful nature, the Law and the Prophets demanded the ultimate penalty: death. Here we begin to see the foreshadowing of the path Jesus is calling us to, the path that leads to the cross.

The very grace that led Christ to suffer death for our sake is the same grace that is extended to us every day as we clumsily and imperfectly attempt to be his salt and light to the world. This is not a license to sin or to remain casual in our commitment to righteousness and justice. Far from it! In fact, it is the unparalleled nature of that mercy and grace that drives us to ever deeper devotion, humility, repentance, sacrifice, service and love, both to God and to others. Otherwise we use Christ's entire life, including his brutal suffering and death, as a convenience against our own casual pattern of selfishness and sin, crucifying him anew each time. Instead, we are called to obediently take up our cross daily and die to our sin, humbled at the unmerited gift it represents.

To that end, Little Flowers Community strives (albeit imperfectly) to live in daily accountability to God and each other. We choose to trade our "rights" to privacy and personal faith for the hard disciplines of confession and correction. We nurture trust and intimacy that allow us to speak into each other's lives, even in the discomfort of very painful and personal issues. Is it easy? Of course not. Are we always willing? Far from it. However, we are convinced that if we are going to see God's kingdom break forth in our community, then it is going to have to start in our lives and our hearts. Perhaps, in this respect, we are blessed to be in a context where our sin and brokenness is so much more apparent. It is one of the most difficult and rewarding things I have ever been a part of. After all, we cannot have resurrection without the cross.

THREE GREAT SINS

When Jesus declared the Law and the Prophets were fulfilled in him, that we were not to reject, ignore or even minimize their ultimate expectations, he was doing so through the lens of a people who had been transformed into salt and light. He went on to name three incredibly high-profile sins that the law clearly forbade at great consequence: murder, adultery and divorce. While he was in no way intending for this to be his definitive teaching on the topics, he was pulling no punches in choosing them as his prime examples to illustrate his wider meaning.

Murder. The prohibition against murder was a law that few of Jesus' listeners would have broken, as it is likely to be a law that very few of us have broken either. Here, however, he recast the sin into terms that no one, then or now, was guiltless of.

> You have heard that it was said to the people long ago, "Do not murder, and anyone who murders will be subject to judgment." But I tell you that anyone who is angry with his brother will be subject to judgment. Again, anyone who says to his brother, "Raca," is answerable to the Sanhedrin. But anyone who says, "You fool!" will be in danger of the fire of hell.
>
> Therefore, if you are offering your gift at the altar and there remember that your brother has something against you, leave your gift there in front of the altar. First go and be reconciled to your brother; then come and offer your gift. (Matthew 5:21-24)

Jesus reminds us with powerful clarity that the law is not kept through external and explicit obedience to prescribed behaviors or adherence to a set of prohibitions, such as *not* murdering people. Rather, we see that the bar of righteousness has been raised significantly, requiring that we not only follow the law in its prohibitions but also in its ultimate intentions, writing them on our very hearts. The measure of our obedience to the law, then, is as much about our inner motives and intentions as it is about our actions. Further, it is as much about the good we fail to do as it is about the evil we resist (James 4:17). And only a people of humbled righteousness, as found in the Beatitudes, can ever hope for such purity of heart.

Here it is helpful for us to better understand the meaning of the word for "sin" used in the New Testament. One of the Greek words for sin, *hamartanō*, literally means "to miss the mark," suggesting that sin is more about what we've missed—what we've failed to be and do—than about the transgression itself (though God is very concerned with that as well). Murder is wrong, ultimately, because it is a failure to be loving, peaceful, patient, gracious, merciful and just. That is why Jesus says that simply resisting the sinful act does not free us from the indictment of the law, for it demands a heart transformed by righteousness and justice. The active love of God and the love of others must be a product of those transformed hearts.

Jesus makes an interesting shift at this point. Having established that our hearts indict us as much (and perhaps more so) than our actions, he shifts perspectives from being the one who has anger toward others, to being the target of others' anger. Why this change? Dewi Hughes explains Jesus' intentions:

> He assumes that the sort of persons described in the Beatitudes will not harbor hatred against others, so that they are free to try and deal with the hatred directed against them. . . . Our calling as kingdom people is to do everything in our power to change the hearts of our enemies.[1]

As ones called to be the community of the Beatitudes, not only are we meant to have hearts transformed by God's grace and mercy (thus free from such things as hatred), but our primary responsibility is to be the preserving salt and life-giving light to others. In other words, even at our own expense, whether we are in the right or the wrong, our first priority is to guard the other person from the corruption of sin, bringing life instead through acts of humility, generosity and grace. That he calls us to do so even before we come before him in worship, something far more significant to the Jewish people than it is to most of us today, underlines the deep significance and importance this kind of commitment has. For as we do this, resisting the impulse to accuse, to defend and to justify, we demonstrate the fulfillment of God's intention and allow the shalom of his kingdom to break through just a little bit more. Perhaps this is what Jesus meant in John 15:13 when he said, "Greater love has no one than this, that he lay down his life for his friends." While clearly a foreshadowing of his own sacrifice for us on the cross, I believe that he also meant that in our indivisible commitment to love God and others, every part of our life must be given up (even unto death) for the sake of God's mission to the world. This is what it means to love our neighbors as ourselves.

Adultery. Living in a neighborhood known for its very active sex trade, I have seen far too many minivans with baby seats and Jesus-fish bumper stickers picking up prostitutes to think that adultery is as uncommon as many would believe. Therefore it is no surprise to me that Jesus strikes at another hot topic, one that would hit closer to home for more people than murder had. He continues to show that we are not made righteous by external acts of obedience, demonstrating that it is not merely the external act of adultery that qualify as sin, but the very intentions of the heart.

> You have heard that it was said, "Do not commit adultery." But I tell you that anyone who looks at a woman lustfully has already committed adultery with her in his heart. If your right eye causes you to sin, gouge it out and throw it away. It is better for you to lose one part of your body than for your whole body to be thrown into hell. And if your right hand

causes you to sin, cut it off and throw it away. It is better for
you to lose one part of your body than for your whole body
to go into hell. (Matthew 5:27-30)

Regarding Jesus' command about the disposal of our sinful eye
or hand, I was always taught that Jesus was overstating the case to
demonstrate how seriously he takes sin; he obviously was not
being literal.

What if he was, in fact, being literal—deadly serious and absolutely literal? You see, Jesus knew that neither our eyes nor our
hands, nor any part of our body, for that matter, can ever *cause* us
to sin, but rather that only our hearts have that power. And it is
our hearts—our minds, our emotions and our will—that lead us
into sin, and therefore it is our hearts that must be cut out. It is in
daily dying to ourselves, to our sinful hearts, that we will find
freedom and new life, and we are invited to join Christ as the only
way in which such a new life is possible. Just as in the Beatitudes
we are led to the culmination of suffering with Christ, so too does
death offer not a defeat but a paradoxical hope. Our dependence
on God's grace in this is absolute.

Divorce. Then Jesus admonishes:

It has been said, "Anyone who divorces his wife must give
her a certificate of divorce." But I tell you that anyone who
divorces his wife, except for marital unfaithfulness, causes
her to become an adulteress, and anyone who marries the
divorced woman commits adultery. (Matthew 5:31-32)

All too often Jesus' teaching on the subject of divorce has been
used as a definitive text on the subject. Those who use his words
in this way negligently ignore the fullness of what Scripture has to
say about the topic and defeat the very point Jesus is trying to
make using this illustration. It was not Jesus' intention to make
this the all-encompassing ethic on marriage and divorce, and neither is it my intention here. Having walked with family and friends

through the tragic dynamics of divorce, I believe it would be a disservice and dishonor to them and to God to represent this section as if it were definitive on the topic. That being said, Jesus' use of this example is important for us to understand.

Jesus was confronting a very real problem among the Jews of his day. Using the letter of the law (often stretching it with extreme creativity), men were finding ways to free themselves from marriage. For whatever reason, they wanted to be released from the God-ordained covenant with their wives, but also freed of any moral or legal responsibilities for doing so. They were exploiting the law—whose intentions were to bring about a righteous and just kingdom—for their own selfish desires. The laws surrounding divorce were designed to protect us and instill in us the true meaning of faithful love of God and others. To use it in such a way was becoming all too common and was a violation of the spirit in which the law was given, and thus a violation of the law itself. The sanctity of faithfulness in covenant, reflected in and through marriage, spoke to the deeper sanctity in the covenant that God extended to all of us. In fact, this abuse created a dynamic of injustice toward these rejected wives (and thus women in general) that produced the very antithesis of the just kingdom the law was meant to produce. Again, the letter of the law was not at issue, but the true intention of the heart was exposed.

UNENFORCEABLE OBLIGATIONS

Using these powerful examples of murder, adultery and divorce, Jesus calls his community to be a people no longer defined simply by an avoidance of sin, but rather one in which "what is avoided is so because of the character of the community that is to exemplify Christ's life."[2] In other words, the nature of our transformed hearts and lives makes it so that we are a community of peacemaking, of reconciliation and shalom. If we are truly defined by these virtuous reflections of Christ, then the prohibitions of the law are transformed into a vision of a better world, his kingdom, which has been inaugurated by Christ and continues to break forth in our lives.

In these three examples, Jesus left no one untouched. Even the righteousness of the Pharisees, who attempted to prove their godliness through purely external and compromised adherence to the law, was proven inadequate and reprehensible before God. However, before the common people could rejoice that their so-called spiritual superiors had been taken down a peg, Jesus warned them that this did not lower the bar and thus make their relative righteousness more acceptable. Instead, he showed them the impossibly high standard to which God calls all his people—impossible, that is, apart from his grace and mercy and the power of his Spirit. While he pointed to a life of demanding and radical obedience, he did so in a way that was full of hope and promise.

In the midst of the American civil rights movement in the 1960s, Dr. Martin Luther King Jr., in addition to his activism, continued to serve in his vocation as a pastor. He recognized that his political activism could not be divorced from his faith in Christ. When preaching on the U.S. government's attempts at desegregating society, he once said:

> Morality cannot be legislated, but behavior can be regulated.
> . . . Desegregation will break down the legal barriers and bring men together physically, but something must touch the hearts and souls of men so that they will come together spiritually because it is natural and right. A vigorous enforcement of civil rights laws will bring an end to segregated public facilities, which are barriers to a truly desegregated society, but it cannot bring an end to fear, prejudice, pride, and irrationality, which are barriers to a truly integrated society.
>
> These dark and demonic responses will be removed only as men are possessed by the invisible, inner law which etches

on their hearts the conviction that all men are brothers and that love is mankind's most potent weapon for personal and social transformation. True integration will be achieved by true neighbors who are willingly obedient to unenforceable obligations.[3]

Many Christians decry the state of our culture, where murder, infidelity and divorce are just a few of the sins we see running rampant around us. Our impulse to retreat into the stability and security of tightly defined laws with clear and effective consequences is understandable. This critical posture is one that many people immediately identify as what it means to be a Christian. Yet, as Dr. King clearly understood in the teaching and example of Jesus, it is in the transformation of hearts, not the legislating of behavior, that true change takes place.

Living in that tension is far more difficult than it sounds. As a community of the faithful, how do we remain vigilant to how easily sin corrupts our hearts—even before it is expressed in our actions—without resorting to guilt tactics and strict rules? At Little Flowers we struggle with this daily, confronted by both our own brokenness and the brokenness in our neighborhood. We know that it is only possible to live this way through the grace and forgiveness of Christ, and so we have also begun to practice that grace and forgiveness with one another. Instead of focusing our attention on the sins of our sister or brother, we are committed to being mindful of our own sin—not dealing with it as an issue of personal piety but confessing it to each other, praying and supporting one another in the midst of it. It is here where the sins hidden in our hearts are brought into the light, exposed and forgiven before they take root in our lives. This has continually been the most difficult, messy and rewarding discipline in our community.

Oaths, Eyes and Enemies

Matthew 5:33-48

I was furious. For perhaps the dozenth time Bill had promised to get something done, to organize the group to help get the community house cleaned and ready for ministry, only to sit around like the cool guy, playing cards and chatting. No matter how clearly we told him, no matter how many times he promised to do it, the result was always the same: nothing got done. Since many of us share life together in intentional community, these responsibilities were critical to maintaining the household and healthy relationships. Resentment was growing among those who had to, in addition to their own responsibilities, cover Bill's as well. I had had enough. Approaching the table where they were all sitting and chatting, I quietly asked him what they had finished doing from the list of tasks. He waved me off, telling me it would get done. I insisted and again he brushed it off, telling me not to even worry about it. That is when I lost it.

Right there in front the whole group, I tore into him. I let him have it, telling him exactly what his irresponsibility cost the rest of us and reminding him that his commitment as a leader was not only to get his responsibilities dealt with but also to model maturity and servanthood to those he led. I pointed out every excuse he had lamely given over the last few weeks, sarcastically asking how such simple tasks could confound him for so long. I was at the height of righteous indignation, and he felt the full weight of my wrath. Leaving him in stunned silence with every eye in the room on him, I stormed out.

And I was immediately sick to my stomach.

No matter if I was right about the situation, and no matter if Bill was wrong for his failures, what I had just done was unacceptable and I knew it. Kim soon found me and gently asked what had happened. I retold the story, stressing how frustrated everyone was with Bill. My wife nodded in genuine understanding, then said, "You know you are going to have to apologize, right? To Bill and to the group." I hated to hear it, but I knew she was right. It was inappropriate, unkind and inexcusable. I would have to apologize to Bill and the whole group, just as Kim had pointed out. The worst of it, though, was that my apology was going to have to be as public as my outburst and it would have to be free of any excuses. Every time I thought through what I would say, I would catch myself trying to qualify my apology, to minimize my failings in light of Bill's faults. I realized that this would ultimately disqualify my very apology, so I swallowed my pride, despite how unfair it seemed to me.

In the end, I did make a public apology, painfully with no qualifications or veiled accusations against Bill. Bill came off as the gracious brother in Christ, magnanimously extending his forgiveness to me. In truth, he was very gracious in light of how I had treated him. I wish I could say that such an act of humble submission to the greater good left me with a feeling of spiritual bliss or even simple peace, but the truth was that it ate at me for months to come. Even now, years later, I find myself gritting my teeth at the memory of it. Whoever said "Doing good is its own reward" had a sick sense of humor. Of course, in the end, I am glad I did what I did. At the time I was in a position of authority where people had to place a great deal of trust in me, and that trust needed to be proven out by my character. They had to see that when I made mistakes—and they saw plenty of those—I not only would take responsibility but would do so without excuse or complaining. In many ways that experience helped set a tone of trust and honesty for the rest of the time that community was together.

OATHS

Having confronted our tendency to artfully interpret the law, seeking out loopholes and weaknesses, Jesus continues confronting our sinful compromises. The tension within me to try to find a way to both take responsibility for my own failings and expose Bill's failing (ultimately to justify myself and my behavior) is the same tension being addressed by Jesus in his admonition about taking oaths. Old Testament laws made clear allowance for making oaths or vows, though the vast majority of these laws warned against abusing or reneging such vows. In Jesus' time, the teachers of the law and the rabbis had devised creative interpretations that allowed them to place emphasis on the formulation of the oaths rather than on the underlying intention of the warning. Essentially, they decided that only vows made explicitly in the name of God were binding, so it was no sin to break any other oaths. Like in my response to Bill, they wanted to find a way to remain faithful to God yet still reap the benefits of their own personal desires.

For the community of the crucified, such distinctions will never work. Jesus explains:

Again, you have heard that it was said to the people long ago, "Do not break your oath, but keep the oaths you have made to the Lord." But I tell you, Do not swear at all: either by heaven, for it is God's throne; or by the earth, for it is his footstool; or by Jerusalem, for it is the city of the Great King.

And do not swear by your head, for you cannot make even one hair white or black. Simply let your "Yes" be "Yes," and your "No," "No"; anything beyond this comes from the evil one. (Matthew 5:33-37)

The law does not primarily exist to warn us about the evil which we are called to avoid but to point us to the light which exposes such sin to the revelation of the greater goodness of Christ and his kingdom—to this all the Law and the Prophets point. Further, because Jesus is the very fulfillment of the law, it is impossible to formulate a vow within that law apart from doing so in the name and presence of God. "The earth is the LORD's, and everything in it, the world, and all who live in it" (Psalm 24:1), therefore nothing can be sworn upon in all of creation that is not, ultimately, in the name of God. All vows, regardless of what they are sworn upon, are binding as though before God; thus vows ultimately become unnecessary. The community of the Beatitudes is such that the only oath to their honesty is the proven character demonstrated in their evident work of being salt and light.

After all, what do oaths suggest except that whenever we do *not* swear by one, our words are then questionable? In other words, if we must swear to our truthfulness in one circumstance, all other circumstances where we fail to make such oaths become suspect. Or conversely, by swearing especially to the truth in one situation, our word might be suspicious, because we "protest too much."[1] Therefore, we know that what is ultimately at stake here is not the use of oaths but rather the condition and truthfulness of our heart. Jesus is not making a prohibitive law against making oaths to replace the prohibitive laws about the proper use of oaths, for he would simply be replacing one external rule for another. After all, having likened calling our brother a fool with being worthy of the fires of hell, Jesus later rebukes the Pharisees, calling them "blind fools" (Matthew 23:17). And when being questioned by the chief priest and the Sanhedrin, the only question Jesus willingly answered was the one leveled at him "under oath by the living God" (Matthew 26:62-64). Jesus' point, it is therefore clear, is not to set up a new and revised set of external rules that we must adhere to, but rather to again show us that the difference is in our hearts.

As we become, by his grace and his Spirit, the community of the Beatitudes—the community of the crucified—as we truly and actively participate with his mission as the salt of the earth and light of the world, the truthfulness of our character will be proven by our lives of humble mercy and selfless justice poured out for others, even at and especially at our own expense. This unparalleled integrity of heart is the expected standard for all Christians at all times, in circumstances great and small. For it is our lives that now become the living oaths to the credibility of God and his emerging kingdom. When we violate that integrity, not only is our own character stained but we dishonor and discredit the God and gospel we represent. Faithfulness in being truthful is a reflection of the single-minded allegiance we are to have for God. It is the very nature of being pure in heart. Any compromise in our truthfulness, then, is a betrayal of that allegiance and must come from the evil one, for we can have but one master.

However, it is not just to other people that we are prone to swear such oaths. I suspect all of us can think of many times when we cried out to God in response to a trial or temptation. Whether it was of our own making or not, most of us have found ourselves swearing to God that, should he just intercede in our circumstances, we would respond with a gratitude proven through special devotion and obedience to him. While we are of course meant to call on God in times of suffering and need, we are never to do so by swearing oaths to God as compensation. How can we offer as payment for his intercession an obedience that is already absolutely and unequivocally owed him? Are we not already his servants in entirety? It is pure arrogance for us to bargain with what isn't even our own! What an insult to offer to God, in exchange for his intervention, what is already his. The insult is double, for not only is our faithfulness not ours to bargain with but the very loving intervention and provision we seek is promised us by him already as his beloved children. Therefore, our words should be few, and when we use them, they should be the truth of our heart, unembellished and unqualified. Let our yes be yes and our no, no.

EYE FOR AN EYE

In St. Francis's day the protection of the law was largely centered in the larger towns and cities. As a result, the areas outside those cities were often plagued by bandits who preyed on unprotected travelers. Assisi was no exception. Once, while Francis was away, a group of bandits confronted and threatened the other friars, demanding that they give them something to eat. Brother Angelo boldly stepped forward and rebuked them: "You wicked men! It's not enough that you would shamelessly rob others of the fruits of their hard labor, but now you have the audacity to demand food from us friars—food designated to support the servants of God! You should be ashamed!"

Angry and insulted, but ultimately fearing God's judgment, the bandits left empty-handed.

Later that day, when Francis returned, he was carrying a sack of bread and a jug of wine that had been given to him to share among the brothers. When Angelo proudly told Francis of his brave rebuke, he was shocked to find that it made Francis very upset. "How could you have acted so cruelly to our brothers?" Francis demanded. "You know that sinners are more likely to return to the Father though meekness than a harsh scolding. Have I not made it clear? 'Let whoever may approach us, whether friend or foe, thief or robber, be received kindly.'"

Taking the sack of bread and jug of wine, the only food available to the brothers that day, Francis gave them to Angelo and commanded him to find the robbers. He was to offer them the bread and wine, begging on bended knees for their forgiveness for his cruel rejection. Once he had done that, he should then admonish those men to refrain from thievery and violence, to fear God and to love their neighbors. Francis commanded Angelo to tell the robbers that if they would cease their wickedness, he would take care of all their needs in the future. While Brother Angelo went in search of the bandits, Francis prayed and begged the Lord to soften the hearts of the bandits and turn them toward repentance.

Upon finding the robbers, Angelo did all that Francis had commanded—he fed them, repented of his cruelty, encouraged them to change their ways and promised that if they did, Francis would care for all their needs. As they ate their food in front of the humbled and hungry friar, the men were convicted of their selfish and violent ways. They returned to Francis with Angelo, ready to start a new life of obedience to God to the astonishment of all the brothers.

Francis understood what Jesus meant when he said, "You have heard that it was said, 'Eye for eye, and tooth for tooth.' But I tell you, Do not resist an evil person" (Matthew 5:38-39). Having cautioned us against abusing the law for our own personal agendas or convenience, Jesus goes on to say that, even when we are the victim of others' unrighteousness, we are to live in the present blessings he describes. Francis knew that the sin of greatest significance was that which is in our own hearts. Again, if our unrighteousness is proven by the condition of our hearts, then whether we are committing the sin or suffering from the sins of others, the standard does not change.

The Old Testament concept of "an eye for an eye" sounds barbaric to modern readers. People are fond of quoting Gandhi who said, "An eye for an eye leaves the whole world blind." However, what it represented was a moral and judicial code that helped govern the fair punishment for sin. If a person lost his eye by an-other, this code was not suggesting that the perpetrator should also lose an eye. Rather, it said that the compensation owed the suffering person was to be equivalent to the value of the eye. Be-fore this was in place, revenge and retaliation were rampant. If a man lost an eye by his neighbor, he would kill his neighbor in response. The neighbor's family would then retaliate by killing the man's whole family, and so the cycle would go. "An eye for an eye," then, was a very progressive and necessary law that still shapes compensatory laws worldwide.

This is important for us to note because Jesus isn't rejecting an unfair or brutal system of vindication here but actually the very sys-tem of fair compensation that most of us take for granted today. Jesus is not seeking to reject or replace one law with another one, where we are now contractually obligated to do the specific things listed in his teaching. Rather, he is reminding us again that sin is not defined by the evil acts or intentions themselves, but by the right-eousness they fail to support. Remember, the peacemakers—those dedicated to bringing reconciliation and wholeness as their first pri-ority—are the ones who see God. In other words, God is all they see because he is all that is left. Their own agendas, rights and desires are gone, so they're left only with a desire to be his salt and light.

> The followers of Jesus for his sake renounce every personal right. He calls them blessed because they are meek. If after giving up everything else for his sake they still wanted to cling to their own rights, they would then have ceased to follow him. This passage therefore is simply an elaboration of the beatitudes.[2]

When nothing but the love of God and the love of others is in our hearts, we no longer need to vie for our own self-interest when faced with these situations but rather can focus on the greater good that is the heart of the other. Not only does this selfless willingness to sacrifice more than is required or merited demonstrate the extravagant and generous love of God, but it is the only indictment against violence that does not propagate yet more violence (at least not without further exposing their own sin). Once again we see that the community of the Beatitudes must also be the community of the crucified, willing to pay any price for God's kingdom to break forth in the world and, perhaps, even in the hearts of our enemies.

> I tell you, Do not resist an evil person. If someone strikes you on the right cheek, turn to him the other also. And if someone wants to sue you and take your tunic, let him have your cloak as well. If someone forces you to go one mile, go with him two miles. Give to the one who asks you, and do not turn away from the one who wants to borrow from you. (Matthew 5:39-42)

By using the three examples he does—being struck in the face, being taken to court for our tunic and being required by the Roman army to carry their gear for a mile—Jesus quickly shuts down any idea that this is merely an ethic for personal conflict resolution. While the first example is certainly a personal one, the second is an example of a public and legal conflict, and the third an example of a social, governmental or even military conflict. The heart of the law, fulfilled in Christ perfectly on the cross, is to be fulfilled in our own hearts and lives in every respect. There is to be no division between our personal, professional and political lives. Dietrich Bonhoeffer notes, "This distinction between person and office is wholly alien to the teaching of Jesus. He is the Lord of all life, and demands undivided allegiance."[3]

Jesus is the fulfillment of all of the Law and the Prophets. That fulfillment found its truest expression on Golgotha, on the cross. On that same cross we are to be transformed into his children, reflecting his uncompromising love for all creation. It is to this cross of suffering and death that we invite the world, for it is there that the only hope for salvation is found. How then, in the face of our own suffering, can we not follow Christ's teaching in this matter? Unless our obedience is such that we are willing to take up our cross daily in this way, we make the cross a happy myth, empty of all meaning and power.

In a time when Christians are desperate to make the faith look attractive and relevant, such a commitment can seem counterintuitive. Little Flowers Community has known its fair share of suffering and difficulty, some of it of our own making. We are committed to facing together the demands of following Christ and the hard life that requires, resisting the impulse to dress up the faith to make it more appealing. I know that we could increase our attendance with some high-energy worship music or a creative children's program, and while there is nothing inherently wrong with either of those things, given who we are as a community and the resources at our disposal, we would be sacrificing what matters in the hope that we could appeal to a certain consumer demographic. Don't get me wrong, being a part of Christ's community is (or should be) very attractive, very fulfilling and full of very real joy. However, we endeavor to present the beauty of his church as it is born authentically out of our hearts rather than simply mimicking the external representations that we think it should take.

LOVE YOUR ENEMIES

Up until this point Jesus was demonstrating the radical nature of the Law and the Prophets as they were fulfilled through him and made manifest through his community of the crucified. Now he introduces the capstone of his kingdom explicitly for the first time: love. And more than this, he calls us to love in the most extraordinary way—to love our enemies. Consider the implications of this: the first time Jesus ever teaches about love—that characteristic so central to God's nature that he is explicitly identified with it (1 John 4:8)—he calls us to *love our enemies!* Before Jesus "loves the little children," before he "loves me, this I know," he calls us to be a people formed by a love for our enemies. What staggeringly offensive and beautiful grace!

And we are not simply to love people whom we declare as enemies, for by now it is clear that there is no room for hatred or malice in the hearts of true citizens of his kingdom. We have but one enemy, and it is not of flesh and blood. No, we are to love those who, in the face of the radical life of the Beatitudes we seek to embody, call *us* their enemy. We are to love those who insult us, persecute us and say all kinds of evil against us because of Christ. This is no abstract concept of love, nor is it condescending pity, but a love that would seek their very best even as they take from us our very last breath. Just as Christ, from the entirely undeserved and brutal suffering of his crucifixion, was able to love us enough to declare, "Father, forgive them, for they do not know what they are doing," so too must we love without reserve, without excuse and without any expectation.

> You have heard that it was said, "Love your neighbor and hate your enemy." But I tell you: Love your enemies and pray for those who persecute you, that you may be sons of your Father in heaven. He causes his sun to rise on the evil and the good, and sends rain on the righteous and the unrighteous. If you love those who love you, what reward will you get? Are not even the tax collectors doing that? And if you greet only your brothers, what are you doing more than others? Do not even pagans do that? Be perfect, therefore, as your heavenly Father is perfect. (Matthew 5:43-48)

What does it mean to love? Jesus is very clear about this, saving us from the risk of thinking that love is only some sentiment we must feel for those who call us enemy or from the rationalization whereby we perpetuate violence for their "ultimate greater good" in the name of love. Rather, he shows us again that out of pure hearts flows an active love that touches every aspect of our lives. Standing before our enemies, having relinquished our right to fight back in kind or even defend ourselves, we are called to demonstrate our love for our persecutors by praying for them. Consider the implications of that. True love means that we will stand between them and the judgment of God, which they fully deserve, and plead with God in their defense. We are to be for our enemies—the very people who least deserve or desire our love—what Christ is for us, who are even more undeserving of his love. What a magnificent, terrible and beautiful image of love! Imagine a world in which Christians truly lived this way, not only in the face of the threat of death, but in every moment in every relationship. If this is the love we must have for our enemies, what could surpass it? This is the love we are to have for everyone, just as it is the love that Christ so freely gives to all.

Love. It is toward this end that Jesus has been leading us all along. It is at the heart of his intentions from the dawn of creation and guides us to his final work. Love. Far from mere affection or attraction or loyalty, it is the inconceivable grace in which we are unable and unwilling to distinguish between sister and executioner. Love. It is the offensive grace in which we would extend the hope of forgiveness to both the child and the molester. Love. It is the unparalleled grace in which we find ourselves willing to give even our very lives for others with only a hope, but no promise, that they will repent. Love. It is the cross of Christ. It is *Christ*.

When Little Flowers came to verse 48, we were all quite uncomfortable: "Be perfect, therefore, as your heavenly Father is perfect." However, we discovered the word *perfect* was better translated "complete," "whole" or even "undivided." We are all too aware that we are incomplete, broken and divided. We realized that we are made whole in love, for God's love is absolute and undivided. Beyond the romanticism of loving one another in that shallow, back-patting way, loving each other has not been easy. In my role as a pastor to the community, I have all too often been impatient, unkind, arrogant, selfish and lazy. Yet, without ignoring or diminishing my failing, my community has loved me anyway, correcting me when I need it and forgiving me when I don't deserve it. Between us we've probably had as many conflicts as celebrations, but just as iron sharpens iron (Proverbs 27:17), it is precisely in facing those challenges with love that we become more and more like Christ each day.

Hiding in Plain Sight

Matthew 6:1-8, 16-18

Be careful not to do your "acts of
righteousness" before men, to be seen by them.
If you do, you will have no reward from
your Father in heaven.

MATTHEW 6:1

When Little Flowers Community first wrestled through Jesus' warning about not doing works of righteousness before others, we were puzzled. Half the group asked simultaneously: "Didn't Jesus *just* say that we were supposed let our good works shine before men? Now he is telling us to do it in secret, so that no one will see it. What gives?" Immediately, the story of how we met Jimmy came to mind.[1]

Winnipeg is known for its cold winters. In fact, among urban centers of more than half a million people, it is the coldest city in the world. And given our northern location, the winter sun often sets well before 5 p.m., meaning that by the time we are gathering for our weekly Sunday dinner and worship, people are rushing into our house to escape the bitterly cold darkness. It was during this harsh winter weather that Jimmy first began to hang out with us. Jimmy was a young homeless wanderer who hitch-hiked back and forth across the country. Friendly and funny, he also struggled with an untreated mental illness that could sometimes confuse him. And so, in his own unique logic, he decided to camp out in Winnipeg.

Jimmy made himself at home in our small community. While he did not identify as a Christian, he found Little Flowers Community to be a welcoming (if unusual) group of Christians who treated him more like a family member than a cause for charity or a target for conversion. He would even stick around after the meal to participate in our time of worship and teaching, adding unexpected insights into many topics, especially in respect to loving the poor and practicing true hospitality. Not always comfortable with all aspects of faith, he would respectfully decline to participate at times. Once, when we were taking Communion together, he declined, saying, "I like Jesus and all, I'm just not into eating the guy." Jimmy became a part of our community, someone whom we always looked forward to seeing, whether it was on Sunday evening or anytime during the week.

One particularly cold January night, after the last of the group had headed home, leaving a few of us who live in the community house to do some final clean-up, I noticed Jimmy talking animatedly on the phone. After he hung up, he looked distressed as he went to get his shoes and backpack. Kim immediately asked if everything was all right. It turned out that a friend, who had offered earlier in the day to give Jimmy a place to crash for the night, had rescinded the invitation. With temperatures dropping and the wind-chill factor hitting a deadly -60°F, Brenden, one of the single men who lives in the community house, offered him the couch for the night.

In the end, after working out the details, Jimmy ended up moving in with us for several months while he worked to get things together for the long term. Though Jimmy has since moved on to another city, he remains a good friend who still visits on occasion. We continue to call him friend (staying in touch thanks to modern technology) and pray for him regularly. None of us who know Jimmy could imagine our lives without him. He helped shape our community during its infancy in ways that we will forever be grateful for. Had Brenden been uncomfortable with the arrangement that cold January night, we would not have had such an experience.

> So when you give to the needy, do not announce it with trumpets, as the hypocrites do in the synagogues and on the streets, to be honored by men. I tell you the truth, they have received their reward in full. (Matthew 6:2)

We were helped in processing Jesus' paradoxical command by remembering our experience with Jimmy. Many of us had begun our ministry in the inner city with a heart to serve the poor, to feed the hungry and to clothe the naked. Though well-intentioned, some people even admitted to dreaming about becoming the "Shane Claiborns of Canada." It was not hard for any of us to see how easily our passion for serving God and others can get clouded with selfish and prideful motivations. Yet when we welcomed Jimmy into our home and into our lives, we were not motivated by the prestige such an action might earn us or by some religious obligation to get in our quota of service to the poor. Rather, we were motivated by the love of wanting what was best for someone whom we called friend and who faced an unthinkable alternative. We loved Jimmy, and so we did what needed to be done. It was that simple.

Recently, something else struck me in light of this subject: While it is true that our welcome of Jimmy into our home was the natural response to a friend in need, the truth is that far too many

Christians, while very willing to participate in this kind of radical hospitality, do not live in such a way (or such a place) that such friendships are even possible. It is not enough to wait for such relationships to form, but rather we must alter our lives in such a way that such friendships are possible. Too many Christian communities live in comfortable isolation from the very people God calls us to call neighbor and friend. As I mentioned earlier in reference to Deuteronomy 15:4, when God said that "there should be no poor among you," he wasn't suggesting segregation.

SECRET RIGHTEOUSNESS

Jesus continued the Sermon on the Mount: "When you give to the needy, do not let your left hand know what your right hand is doing, so that your giving may be in secret. Then your Father, who sees what is done in secret, will reward you" (Matthew 6:3). So how should we understand these secret works of righteousness? Interestingly, the Greek word used for "acts of righteousness" in verse 6:1 is not the same word in every manuscript. Some ancient manuscripts that include this passage use the same word for "righteousness" as is used in the Beatitudes, the righteousness/ justice we are to hunger and thirst for. Other manuscripts, though, use an entirely different word meaning "almsgiving" or simply "gifts to the poor." After shooting off a few e-mails to some Bible scholar friends of mine, I learned that while the best manuscripts use the former meaning (that is, they refer to works of justice), the reason the other meaning is used at times is because the primary "act of righteousness" in the Judaism of Jesus' day was almsgiving.

The use of both Greek words suggests that Jesus was referring to the Jewish practice called *tzedakah*, a Hebrew word that loosely means "charity" but has as its root the Hebrew word for justice (*tzedek*). The word is rooted in the gleaning laws of their agrarian past, though the complexities of the developing economy led to a more sophisticated set of guidelines and requirements about giving to the poor. However, consistent throughout that development was the central fact that such giving was always to be done anonymously. What we can glean, then, is that while Jesus is commenting broadly on works of justice, most of his listeners would have thought immediately of *tzedakah*. And given that Jesus continues by directly addressing the practice of almsgiving in the following section, this connection is obviously intentional.

The connection between righteousness/justice and providing for the poor must not be missed or minimized. Its long history in Judaism and Christianity, and Jesus' clear affirmation of its continued practice, should be more than enough to make us mindful of its significance for the church. As we have explored earlier, it is not uncommon these days for Christians to believe that God calls us to care for the spiritual needs of others, with material needs being a secondary priority (and often a distant second at that). Some even go so far as to say we are not called to meet the material needs of the poor at all. However, most would simply minimize such charity as a secondary, less important aspect to the higher spiritual calling of saving souls.

We cannot miss that Jesus makes no such division or distinction between the spiritual and material needs of humanity. The righteousness and justice we are called to hunger and thirst after, and the shalom we are called to create in the world—even in its brokenness—are absolutely concerned with the whole person, and indeed all of creation. The disintegrative nature of sin is being reversed by the work of Christ's redemption, moving us toward the intended wholeness of creation, reflected in the nature of the Garden of Eden before sin. It was good! Our commitment to Christ and his mission, then, must be equally devoted to the restoration of the whole person and the whole creation.

When we understand the dynamics at work here, we see that Jesus is not teaching anything new in respect to the requirement of giving to the poor (and acts of justice in general), nor are his warnings about doing so to be seen as righteous by those watching us. This was something all good Jews knew to avoid. However, two things distinguish Jesus' admonition. First, Jesus is not forbidding us from doing works of righteousness before others (which would indeed be a contradiction of his earlier mandate), but rather he is warning us against doing such works *for the purpose of being seen by others.* Once again, Jesus is forcing us to examine the intentions of our heart, for the true nature of our righteousness is found there, not in the act itself. We must live in the tension between the interior formation of our hearts and the ethical behavior it gives birth to. We should not be surprised that this was such a common problem in his day. After all, which of us does not like getting praised for our good works? This is a universal temptation that we all face.

Jesus calls such people, with their public displays of so-called righteousness, "hypocrites." This would have been an even more cutting rebuke then than it is today, for in addition to it referring to those whose expressed beliefs were not reflective of their heart, the people would have recognized it as the Greek word for actors or performers. In other words, they were fakes and frauds, pretending to be someone or something they were not; after all, it certainly was not about the recipient of the giving or the God who mandated it, but rather it was about the giver receiving praise and honor for his or her devout generosity. Jesus tells them that their acts will mean nothing to their heavenly Father, but that the passing, fickle praise of others will be their only reward. It is here we see for whom we should be doing such good works. Like a child running with their crayon drawing, shouting, "Look what I made for you, Daddy!" so too should our main motivation in such acts of service be pleasing our heavenly Father, whose love for us is the greatest, truest and only reward we desire. And extending from that love of God, we should be moved by genuine love for others.

The second unique aspect of Jesus' warning is that, while we are not to perform these works of justice for the benefit of on-lookers, we are not called to hide our righteousness from those onlookers. Rather, we are called to hide it from ourselves! How can we hide from ourselves our own actions? Of course, Jesus is not suggesting that we somehow induce a form of regular and persistent amnesia, but instead is showing us that it is not even enough to keep our works of righteousness secret from others, for the true source of the temptation is in our own hearts. How do we overcome such temptations and hide our just deeds from our-selves? Only the pure in heart, who see only God, can hope to find such hiddenness. It is only when, formed into the commu-nity of the Beatitudes, through becoming the community of the crucified, that we are able to love God and our neighbor, free of selfish intentions.

I am not suggesting that any of us will fully achieve a kind of moral perfection. Our sinful nature will time and again cause us to stumble and fail. Jesus is not unaware of this reality. Time and again, he alludes to our need for humble repentance and the means of our redemption. For example, in chapter nine we will look at the Lord's Prayer, in which Jesus includes a prayer of repentance for our sins. This isn't license to sin or an argument against mu-tual accountability but is reflective of the ever-present need for the essential grace of Jesus Christ each day. It is critical to keep this truth central in our hearts and minds while seeking to following Jesus' teachings in the Sermon on the Mount, for otherwise we might think that such obedience can save us or even reflect merit of our own. We would simply be setting up another law we cannot possibly fulfill. Rather, we humbly acknowledge that the impos-sible life to which Jesus calls us is, in fact, possible only by his grace and through the power of his Holy Spirit.

Even today, Jewish worship services quite often close with a call for the people to "perfect the world under the sovereignty of

God." This is understood to mean that by the power of God alone, they are to work to bring the brokenness of the world into God's intended wholeness and completion. The practice of *tzedakah* has always been seen as one central aspect of that work. The goal of our works of justice, then, under the sovereignty of God, are to bring shalom for the sake of others and the glory of God. Jesus was referring to this wholeness and completion in Matthew 5:48, as we explored in chapter seven. And this is achieved through love. Love is the only pure intention for acts of justice—love of God and love of others. We must nurture this love in our hearts if we are to hide our righteousness from even ourselves.

But here's a warning. Not too long ago I had a conversation with a truly well-intentioned young man from our community. All too aware of his own compromised intentions while doing good for others, he had decided to refrain from such activities as volunteering at soup kitchens, donating money to worthy charities and other similar works of justice. His thinking was that until he was able to be free of his selfish intentions, his good works would be worthless anyway. While this young man truly meant well, he was using a dangerous and self-defeating logic. By doing this he was placing his own desire for a pure heart (admirable in and of itself) ahead of the needs of those who were suffering injustice and poverty. His concerns were valid insofar as many good deeds, both those motivated by selfish intentions and those motivated by good intentions, have had a negative impact on the recipients, something the church must be aware of.[2] However, this caution can also result in an equal danger.

Jesus never said that our hypocritical acts of justice would be of no value to the recipients, only that they are of no value to ourselves. Further, he never suggested that our selfish motivations somehow free us of the responsibility of continuing our just works. Making our obedience in good works contingent on some kind of conceptual perfection in our hearts not only perpetuates the injustices that we are called to end, but ultimately suggests that our purity and perfection is something we can achieve by mere effort, apart from the grace and love of God. We must always work at living justly—actively, persistently and immediately—even if our hearts are not yet free of selfish intentions.

HIDDEN PRAYER

Prayer was central to the daily lives of the Jewish people of Jesus' day. Regarding prayer, Jesus taught:

> When you pray, do not be like the hypocrites, for they love to pray standing in the synagogues and on the street corners to be seen by men. I tell you the truth, they have received their reward in full. But when you pray, go into your room, close the door and pray to your Father, who is unseen. Then your Father, who sees what is done in secret, will reward you. And when you pray, do not keep on babbling like pagans, for they think they will be heard because of their many words. Do not be like them, for your Father knows what you need before you ask him. (Matthew 6:5-8)

That Jesus does not mention specially designated hours of prayer is important to note. On the one hand, if he believed they were not necessary or helpful, surely he would have openly taught against them. Therefore, we might conclude that Jesus was not overturning them but explaining or adding to them. On the other hand, if they were important, surely he would have openly affirmed them. Therefore, we might conclude that Jesus was teaching an entirely new way of prayer. What are we to make of this?

Again, it would be wrong for us to assume that Jesus is giving an absolute, definitive teaching on prayer in this section. After all, it is clear that he wasn't rejecting public prayer, because praying together with the community of faith is clearly affirmed elsewhere. And while Jesus rejects babbling on and on with many words, he is not rejecting times of protracted prayer, for he himself spent many long days and nights in prayer. Rather, Jesus is again calling us to examine our intentions in prayer. Where is our heart? And neither is Jesus setting up rules of behavior that we must adhere to explicitly, such as only praying in a room with a closed door. Again, it is not the explicit, external acts that Jesus is immediately concerned with. Rather, he is concerned with them only insofar as they reflect where our hearts are. Bonhoeffer reminds us:

> True prayer is done in secret, but this does not rule out the fellowship of prayer altogether, however clearly we may be aware of its dangers. In the last resort it is immaterial whether we pray in the open street or in the secrecy of our chambers, whether briefly or lengthily, in the Litany of the church, or with the sign of one who knows not what to pray for. True prayer does not depend either on the individual or the whole body of the faithful, but solely upon the knowledge that our heavenly Father knows our needs. That makes God the sole object of our prayers, and frees us from a false confidence in our own prayerful efforts.[3]

Like the works of justice in the previous section, Jesus reminds us that prayer is not to be practiced for the sake of those who might be watching us. Sadly, just as it was then, today we so easily fall into practices that reward such behavior. In wanting to encourage openness and prayer, we can create an environment where people are motivated to be eloquent, to say the right things regardless of where their hearts are. The solution is not to reject public prayer but rather to constantly seek the purity of heart that comes with our singular vision on Christ alone. Might it be helpful for some to refrain from public prayer for a season in order to resist the temptation of performance? Perhaps. But this would be an example of a personal discipline practiced to challenge the heart, not the embrace of an absolute rule or law. At Little Flowers Community we seek to create an environment where prayer is comfortable yet reverent, meaningful yet accessible. Some of us have benefited from praying the Scriptures or using a breviary.[4] We do not utilize different methods out of a consumeristic compromise but out of our pursuit of nurturing genuinely prayerful hearts.

It is not surprising that the lives of the saints centered very strongly around prayer. St. Francis was no exception. Never a scholar, he would spend his time in prayer where others might have been studying—not merely out of a strict religious discipline but because he was driven toward a deep and intimate relationship with God. John Michael Talbot, a Christian musician whose life has been transformed by the Franciscan tradition, finds the ceremony of marriage to be a compelling metaphor for prayer: "In reality, prayer is a mystical union between God and us. It's a form of communication that makes our relationship to God personal and vital. It's not a cold, impersonal ritual, but a warm and loving embrace between the God of the universe and a humble, hungry soul."[5] In the light of such intimacy, praying to be seen by others would be an act of infidelity to Francis, as it should be for us.

It is interesting that Jesus does not abolish the set hours of Jewish prayer (as we see it practiced later by the early church in Acts 3) but rather reminds his listeners that such structures or practices are not the point; they are not the end in and of themselves. Whatever approach we take, the point is that our hearts must be in the right place when we pray—focused on the will and glory of our heavenly Father. Again we see that the God to whom we pray is characterized first and foremost as Father. We pray to him because we love him. Yes, we are obedient and submit to him as our God and King, but our primary motivation in prayer is a loving and active relationship with our most loving Father.

Unlike with the examples of works of righteousness and fasting, Jesus stops in the middle of this teaching on prayer to offer his listeners a quick but revolutionary model for prayer. This teaching on the Lord's Prayer warrants its own chapter. This simple prayer has inspired countless volumes on its meaning. Therefore, it is important that we give it that special attention it deserves. However, it is important to remember that Jesus' teaching here on prayer is not definitive. Prayer is an ancient and beautiful discipline of our faith that spans the full length of human history, requiring from us a lifetime commitment to understanding and practicing it. The point Jesus is making here is to warn us about how easily that commitment can get derailed by our own sinful hearts.

PRIVATE FASTING

Fasting was a familiar and expected practice among the Jewish people listening to Jesus. In addition to the required national fasts—such as Yom Kippur and Tisha B'Av—fasting was a common personal discipline as well. The more devout would voluntarily fast twice a week, on Mondays and Thursdays. The Pharisees were known for keeping these fasts (in part because they went out of their way to make sure everyone knew they were doing it) because it was common and expected among those seen as especially devoted to God.

> When you fast, do not look somber as the hypocrites do, for they disfigure their faces to show men they are fasting. I tell you the truth, they have received their reward in full. But when you fast, put oil on your head and wash your face, so that it will not be obvious to men that you are fasting, but only to your Father, who is unseen; and your Father, who sees what is done in secret, will reward you. (Matthew 6:16-18)

Clearly Jesus is also affirming the practice here, as he did with both giving to the poor and prayer, demonstrated by his admonition on this topic beginning with the words, "When you fast . . ." Fasting, then, is not merely encouraged by Jesus; it is expected.

Yet, unlike giving to those in need and prayer, fasting is far less likely to be practiced by the average Christian today.

When it came to fasting, the hypocrisy of the Pharisees was quite clear to Jesus. When they fasted, they made sure people knew about it. We might dismiss them as arrogantly looking for attention, and some very well might have been motivated to that end. However, we should not overlook the possibility that their public display was an attempt to remind (if not rebuke) others who *should* have been fasting but were not. I remember people from our church who, when eating at a restaurant, would make sure they used body language clearly communicating that they were praying before the meal. They were not arrogant people, but they wanted to demonstrate their commitment and lack of shame at being followers of Jesus to the "nonbelievers" around them. In this way, we cannot dismiss the possibility that the intentions of the Pharisees might have been good. Regardless of their intentions, however, their actions proved them to be hypocrites because that very intention divided their commitment to the true purpose of the discipline.

True and acceptable fasting is a response to God, not an effort to increase our "spiritual status," especially not for the recognition of others. Nor is it meant to be a method to publicly model godliness to others. The outward act is necessary, but it is our response to God, not a means by which we accomplish anything. "Fasting is a *response* to a sacred moment, not an instrument designed to get desired results."[6] We do not fast to prove ourselves holy, to gain the respect of others or even to be a good example of a mature Christian to those who look to us for leadership. Our intentions in fasting (as with any act of Christian devotion or service) must be free from the expectations of results or returns, regardless of how noble they might be. We must put to death any desire for public affirmation, even if we fear others will assume we are impious because they do *not* see us practicing it. Again, we are warned against splitting our allegiance, our devotion, between the one true King and some other master.

Further, even when we fast in secret, we are not doing so in order to receive something from God. Yes, the expectation and hope is there. Yes, God sometimes does offer results. However, that must never be our ultimate purpose or intention, for this simply makes fasting into a manipulative tool by which we hope to extricate from God something for our own benefit and purposes. It is not about turning God to our purposes, but about having our hearts and minds and bodies turned toward him and his purposes. The true quality of our fasting, then, is proven in the condition and intentions of our hearts. Fasting is not proactive or pragmatic but humbly responsive and submissive.

It is not uncommon for Christians today to believe that by denying our physical craving (and need) for food and water, we will receive a heightened sense of spiritual awareness or purity. The conscious or unconscious assumption that somehow our "flesh" is less holy than our "spirit" leads us to believe that if we force one into submission, the other will be free. Because the experience of fasting often does result in significant spiritual experiences and growth, many believe that their assumptions are therefore proven true. However, this simply is not the case. In fact, the truth is quite the opposite. It is the very fact that our being is inseparably physical *and* spiritual that makes fasting so important. Most of Jesus' followers would have found our division of the physical and the spiritual absurd. When we respond to God, we respond with our whole selves. There can be no division.

Proper fasting will not kill us. It won't do us any real harm. Yet when we are faced with the realities of fasting, we resist in powerful ways. Our hunger gets exaggerated. Our minds devise ingenious rationalizations for why we should compromise or quit. It is even all too common for some people to "feel like God has released" them from the obligation. After all, we aren't legalists, are we? In short, fasting is demanding and difficult. It is very often uncomfortable and disempowering. In our culture of rampant self-indulgence, where we feed every craving and pop pills for the most minor of discomforts, it is no wonder that fasting has largely disappeared as a regular Christian discipline in the West. Yet Jesus clearly expects us all to practice it.

It is in the light of the Table of our Lord, in Communion, that fasting takes on its deepest meaning. Christ alone is the Bread of Life, relieving the deepest of hungers. The fleeting fulfillment of food, wealth and power can distract and blind us to the ever-present and universal hunger for that true Bread. Fasting strips us of the pretense that what we have is enough. It liberates us from the illusion that we can make it on our own. It is a powerful and holistic way in which we can practice obedient submission to our Lord and Father. For it is from him that we receive every good thing. Fasting is a bodily response to this truth, beyond a mere intellectual or emotional assertion of its value.

The need for the Christian community in the West to rediscover the importance and appropriate practices of fasting has never been more critical.[7] A great deal has been written, often with good intentions, that distracts and misleads us in the purpose of this discipline. Just as Jesus warned then, so too should we be warned today: unworthy fasting exposes us as hypocrites, dishonoring God among our fellow believers and to a watching world.

Every Sunday evening as we gather as Little Flowers Community, we begin with a potluck meal. As we sit together around the table and share the same food with one another, I am often struck by the reality that apart from the Spirit of Christ this random, ragtag group of people would be unlikely to find themselves in the same room, let alone breaking bread with each other. While we still occasionally practice Communion in more traditional forms, for me these moments are deeply sacred, even in their lack of religious language or ritual. As I satiate my physical hunger, I realize that God is also satisfying a deeper hunger in and through these people who have become my friends, my family. Fasting awakens our hearts and minds to the sacramental reality of a community formed by and in the image of Jesus Christ.

The Disciple's Prayer

Matthew 6:9-15

I should begin by saying that a single chapter is not nearly enough space to explore this beautiful prayer that Jesus gave us. In many ways this prayer is a summation of the entire Sermon on the Mount. For millennia the recitation of this prayer has been a uniting characteristic of Christianity across many traditions, earning the right to have special attention given to it here in the middle of Jesus' great teaching.

You will notice that I have referred to it as "the Disciple's Prayer" instead of the more commonly known Lord's Prayer. I am under no illusion that I am going to reverse the trend of what people call this prayer, nor am I rejecting the traditional title. Rather, I will refer to it here as the Disciple's Prayer because I want to underline its significance and what it teaches in respect to being followers of Jesus Christ. To genuinely pray this prayer and live a life according to its truth is to walk in the way of Christ. By referring to it as the Disciple's Prayer I hope that we will be reminded again that in all things, Jesus is calling us to actively, sacrificially and daily follow him in willing obedience.

OUR FATHER

"Jamie, can I ask you something?" Jimmy was being unusually cautious with me. Generally we could count on him to say what was on his mind, regardless of what it was or how shocking it might be (like the time he asked if any of us had seen the phantom cat-spirit running through our worship service). Now, however, he was clearly hesitant, and so received my full attention immediately. I assured him that he could ask me anything he wanted to, so he cautiously went on.

"Well, I don't want to offend you or say something sacrilegious or anything, but something happened to me. The other night I was riding the bus trying to get some sleep, so I was lying back with my eyes closed. Then I had this feeling that someone was standing over me. I opened my eyes and, umm, well, Jesus was standing over me with his arms spread wide." He looked at me, waiting for a response.

Jimmy was prone to seeing things that weren't there, but usually they were dark terrors that left him in great fear. I had never heard him recount something like this. Clearly, he was not unsettled by this event, so I wanted to hear more. However, when I asked him what he did next, he blushed and looked away.

"That's what I don't want you to be offended by or anything. I mean, I was half asleep so I wasn't trying to be disrespectful or nothing. When I saw him standing there I did the first thing that came to mind. I reached up and tweaked his nipple. You don't think I am going to hell for that, do you?" While I was able to hold back the laugh that was desperately trying to get out, I couldn't suppress my huge grin. I assured him that I thought Jesus would totally understand, affirming that, indeed, I thought he had experienced a genuine encounter with Christ. He was clearly relieved and so continued his story.

"I am glad you said that, because I am pretty sure it was really Jesus too. A couple of nights later, it was getting cold out and my buddy wasn't home, so I needed to find a place to crash for the night. I found a corner in a public parking garage where I could wrap up, but it was getting colder and colder. I remember saying out loud, 'Oh, God, I could use a blanket!' Just as I said that, I felt as though a blanket was being pulled over my body, immediately keeping me warm. No one was there, but I knew right away that it was Jesus. You know how I knew? Because after the invisible blanket was in place, I felt a hand slip down to my chest and tweak my nipple!"

For some, this story might seem to treat the person of Jesus with deep irreverence and disrespect. However, remember that Jimmy sees the world through the cloudy lens of a mental illness that most often leaves him terrified and confused. Anyone who knows him would immediately recognize that this story stands out in stark contrast to the delusions of vampires and demons that typically haunt him. Despite his nipple-tweaking tendencies, I have no doubt that Jesus reached through his illness and revealed himself in a beautiful, tangible way. God repeatedly defies our expectations, humbling himself to meaningfully enter into the brokenness of our lives.

When Jesus began the Disciple's Prayer with the words "Our Father," he did just that. Scholars today generally concede that Jesus would have been using the Aramaic word *abba* for "Father." Two things would have immediately stood out to his disciples. First, he prayed in the common language, not in Hebrew, the sacred language of the Jewish people. It is often lost on us today how significant this was. For the Jews, God's Scripture was always read in Hebrew, and all religious practices, especially prayer, were also in that sacred tongue. This is part of what distinguished the Jews as God's chosen people, set apart from the world for his purposes. When he prayed in Aramaic, Jesus opened the door for all nations to come before God with their own languages (and, by extension, their own cultures). It could even be argued that this was a key shift that contributed to the New Testament being recorded in Greek instead of Hebrew, and thus later into countless other languages around the world.

Second, God was addressed as "Our Father" rather than with the more typical identifiers such as the "God of Abraham, Isaac and Jacob" or other holy titles. While "Our Father" was sometimes used in some formal, traditional prayers, it was less common, and even then was always in Hebrew, clearly establishing that he was the Father of the chosen ones. To make "Our Father" the primary title for God and to do so in the common language of the people was to proclaim that God's fatherhood was to be claimed by all people of all nations, not just by those who were Jewish. This was not a rejection of the Jews by any stretch, but rather the natural fulfillment of his covenant, that through them all nations would be blessed. His intentions for all humans were being fulfilled through Christ, the true Son of God through whom all nations and all of creation would be redeemed.

After Francis sold his father's fabric and horse in an attempt to pay for the repairs to the chapel of San Damiano, his father, Peter Bernadone, was furious. He attempted to have his son arrested and tried as a thief, but the civil authorities could not touch him because he was living in the church. Peter then turned to Bishop Guido, the spiritual leader of Assisi, who summoned Francis to appear before him for judgment, to which he willingly complied. So there, in the piazza in front of the bishop's palace, with the many curious locals watching, Francis was brought before the church authorities. There Peter laid out his accusations against his son: theft of the fabric, theft of the horse, attempting to give the money that did not belong to him to an obscure chapel. The facts were undisputed and Francis did not attempt to defend himself.

Bishop Guido needed very little time to consider. Scolding Francis for his misappropriations and for scandalizing the family name in the process, he ordered the young man to return the money to his father. Not unsympathetic to Francis's newfound zealous faith, he also encouraged him to trust in God for all that he needed. After all, if God wanted him to serve the church, he would certainly provide all that was required. Francis accepted the bishop's judgment without question. Then, unexpectedly, he stepped inside the doors of the palace. Moments later he emerged, and to the shock of everyone present, he was completely naked. He approached his father with the remaining money and all of his clothes, neatly folded, and returned them to their rightful owner. Then, turning to the crowd he said:

> Up until now, I have called this man, Peter Bernadone, my father. However, because I have chosen to serve God, I return to him all his money, as well as all the clothes he provided for me. From this day forward I will no longer call him father, but instead turn to God, my Father who is in heaven.

While Jesus is not asking us all to reject our earthly parents in such a manner, Francis understood in that moment that his truest Father was God, a father who would provide for him all that he needed. Where he once was apprenticed to Peter Bernadone in the trade of selling cloth, he now was apprenticed to his heavenly Father for the purposes of building his kingdom. This young saint understood that by recognizing and submitting to God as his Father, he was not only serving a new master, but entering into a divine, familial bond of grace and love.

For Jimmy this meant that his encounter with Christ reached past mental illness. It reached past the lack of a preexisting foundation of Christian discipleship, and it reached past the unfulfilled expectations of reverence and propriety to connect lovingly to him right where he was at. This is not to say that these things are not important. By no means! Through our continued relationship we have encouraged Jimmy to seek treatment for his illness, to explore and learn more about this Jesus who appeared to him so beautifully, and to learn to follow Christ with all due reverence and respect. But, Jesus subverted the patterns of religious expectation, where people had to align themselves first in wholeness and holiness before they could even presume to approach God. Instead, God reached out even in the midst of our brokenness to declare and demonstrate himself as our loving Father.

We cannot miss the implications this has for our faith communities today. Have we re-created cultures and systems through which a person must navigate in order to approach God? Do we require right behavior or right belief before we "allow" people to encounter God meaningfully? Don't get me wrong; I completely understand why these expectations are in place. I know that the tension of behavior, belief and belonging is a complex dynamic, and that welcoming people into our lives and churches before they believe or behave can be messy and problematic. Nor am I ignoring the dangers that lie with the opposite extreme of requiring nothing at all. I am in no way minimizing these challenges, as they represent a reality that we must live with daily. However, Jesus clearly demonstrates that our emphasis must be to extend ourselves into that complexity to make others feel welcomed as daughters and sons of a loving God, even at our own risk. After all, "while we were yet sinners" Jesus paid the highest price for us with no promise of our gratitude, let alone acceptance. In a way, this foreshadows Pentecost and all the tongues, tribes and nations that will gather before the throne of God to worship him perfectly in unified diversity, a very reflection of the Three-in-One.

Further, when we pray collectively (and it is inarguably clear that Jesus is teaching us a communal prayer) that God is our ultimate and true Father, we must equally affirm the sisterhood and brotherhood we then share with others. While we often affirm this familial relationship with each other in the body of Christ, we must recognize that this is more than a pretty way of telling us to get along; it's a redefining of our primary loyalties and devotions. God is not suggesting that this new spiritual family gives us license to neglect our commitments and obligations to our biological families. It is not about reducing the quality of other commitments and relationships, but rather about elevating these other relationships appropriately in light of our shared, divine Father.

While it is true that the word *abba* is a less formal address for father, it is not entirely accurate to equate it with our conception of "Daddy," as is often done today. It was still a term that carried great authority and respect. The familial name with which we are welcome to address God does not diminish his authority or his worthiness to be revered. For he is our Father who is "in heaven." Rather than a declaration of his location, this is an affirmation that while he is our Father, he is also God. The familiarity we have with God should never cloud or diminish our reverence for him but rather transform it into a reverence born of love and faithfulness, not political or ethnic allegiance, not fear or empty ritual. This must always be held in sacred tension, as we are all too prone to emphasize one or the other of the extremes.

In fact, this calls for a much more binding submission than we might expect. After all, Jesus is the Son of God who looked to the Father for direction in all that he did. In the same way, then, if we are now declaring that God is our Father, our lives must be likewise apprenticed to his will and his ways in all things without exception. It means that we must be always watching for the Father as he's at work in the broken world around us, responding to the painful realities we will see ("blessed are those who mourn"). The very salvation of God's people is tied up with his role as Father, whether it be liberation from the captivity of Egypt or salvation from the tyranny of sin. In other words, by declaring God our Father, we are following Christ's example directly and necessarily to our daily cross in very real and tangible ways.

HIS NAME, HIS KINGDOM AND HIS WILL

While I would never have articulated it this way, I now realize that as a teenager I read the opening lines of the Disciple's Prayer essentially as mere embellishment.

> Hallowed be your name,
> your kingdom come,
> your will be done
> on earth as it is in heaven. (Matthew 6:9-10)

In other words, if we were going to go on to ask God to give us what we wanted—er, needed—we had better butter him up with some praise. Few of us explicitly believe this, but all too often we skim past these opening lines without recognizing their significance. Yet when properly understood they not only teach us a truer understanding of prayer but also what it means to be faithfully part of the community of Christ.

Each declaration in the first half of the prayer calls upon God to bring into being that which only he can accomplish. But implicit in each of these petitions is a call for our submitted participation in his response. It is an affirmation that while no human effort could ever make God's name holy or bring about his kingdom or accomplish his will, by his Spirit he *has* chosen us as his instruments in bringing them about, if only in part. Therefore, to pray these lines is to simultaneously declare our dependence on God while submitting ourselves wholly to be the means by which he accomplishes his purposes. And so we must pay particular attention to these lines, for everything else that follows can only be understood when built on their foundation.

The New Living Translation translates the last part of verse 9 as "may your name be kept holy." When Jesus spoke these words, referencing the name of God, his Jewish listeners would have immediately imagined Moses standing before the burning bush asking God his name. In words that are among the most memorable in both Jewish and Christian traditions, God replies, "I AM WHO I AM" (Exodus 3:14). He reveals himself as the uncreated Creator who was, is and will always be the epitome of holiness. The complex and beautiful history of the name of God in the Judeo-Christian tradition is too great to deal with in this space, but it is critical that we understand the gravity and reverence with which his name was held.[1]

In light of this knowledge, it might seem odd to pray that he would make his name holy. Yet, along with their memories of Moses were their memories of the unfaithfulness that led Israel into exile on more than one occasion. Israel, the chosen people of God, violated their covenant with him and so brought his name into disrepute. Praying that God's name would be made holy (which was not an uncommon prayer in Jesus' day) made a two-fold statement: first, that only by God's grace and mercy might his name be restored through forgiveness of their failings, and second, that they would once again consecrate themselves to lives that only brought glory to him. So too would this line in the Disciple's Prayer carry that double-edged truth for us.

However, now we are to pray as daughters and sons of our Father God. In addition to being subject people who carry his name as our identity, now we also bear it as the family name. In other words, we cannot claim the loving relationship of children to a Father without the requisite commitment that such a relationship brings. Further, like Jesus, we are called to be apprenticed to the purposes of the Father, even unto death. Consider the implications of that level of devotion. Dare we pray these words casually or as a matter of ritual?

As I mentioned earlier, the risk that is all too common for us at Little Flowers Community is reveling in the beauty and liberty that comes with being children of a loving heavenly Father while forgetting the absolute devotion and obedience such a relationship entails. Immediately after learning that we can address God as

Father without the medium of sacred language and culture, we are reminded that it is a privilege received at the cost of our very lives. This remains a difficult tension in our community; we're caught between affirming liberty in defiance of legalism while nurturing a love of God that cannot tolerate compromise of any kind. This is, perhaps, the greatest challenge the church faces every day, seeking faithfulness of the heart without compromise or fear.

Jesus goes on, teaching us to declare, "your kingdom come, your will be done on earth as it is in heaven." This declaration for his kingdom is one that is affirming a distinct future hope. It is a declaration that God will, in human history, fulfill his covenant promises and establish his kingdom in fullness. It holds in its simple, few words the eschatological promise that their suffering would end and that their hopes would be fulfilled. Salvation, in its fullest sense and for all of creation, is working toward completion. And by linking this affirmation with fulfillment on earth in the here and now, Jesus is promising that the blessed kingdom of shalom is breaking through, if only in part, into the world here and now. Even under the devastating rule of a pagan empire, God's kingdom was breaking through. Born out of the hearts of women and men, it is a present reality that defies circumstances and makes us truly blessed.

We are also reminded that God's role as our Father does not diminish his place as our sovereign Lord. These declarations, therefore, are again statements of our active and present submission and devotion to these ends. While declaring that such ends are only God's to accomplish, in that only he is capable, we affirm once more that he chooses to use us as a means to that end, and we therefore give ourselves totally over to him. Total submission to his kingship might have sounded more appealing to Jesus' followers, as they had visions of messianic liberation from Rome at the end of the sword. However, Jesus made clear in the Beatitudes the nature of the kingdom he brings. Further, it is clear what kind of kingdom it is not. Therefore the people knew that this prayer is a call to ultimate humility and sacrifice, to the brokenness of the cross. It was and is the call of a costly kingdom.

The coming of God's kingdom is clearly linked here to the fulfillment of his will. If God is God, King of all creation, then surely his will, will be done. Yet by praying that it will be so, we affirm the beautiful paradox that God has given his subjects freedom to choose. Therefore, like with our submission to his kingship and our dedication to his kingdom, when we pray this prayer we are declaring what Jesus himself would later pray: "Not my will, but yours be done." It is a paradox that we exercise our free will in giving it over entirely to him. Does this mean we no longer have free will? Of course not, no more so than when children whose unwavering love of and faith in their parent leads to their obedience. However, in an age of rights and freedoms, this call to make his will our first and only priority is far more radical than we often realize. He is not calling for the submission of our will only in respect to religious matters, but rather an absolute divestment for the sake of his will. *Blessed are the poor in spirit.*

The repentant and contrite heart of the poor in spirit is critical when we are seeking to discern and obey the will of God. We do ourselves great harm in minimizing or ignoring our capacity to get his will wrong, a lesson repeated time and again. In the complexities of life, demonstrated throughout church history, such endeavors have often led to great failure, even devastating atrocities in the name of God. However, if we allow ourselves to be shaped into the community of the Beatitudes, where we're humbly submitted to God and to one another, led by his Spirit and shaped by his Word, we must believe that God will faithfully guide us. As we have already seen, the community Christ calls us to become is neither perfect nor blind to our failings; we are, rather, a people characterized by humility, repentance and grace.

Few people in history have better understood and embraced

what it means to live these affirmations "on earth as it is in heaven" than St. Francis of Assisi. Today he is often dismissed as a lovable hippy who talked to the animals. Yet this fails to recognize that Francis's love of nature was born out of the conviction that all of creation was to experience the in-breaking kingdom of God. He recognized that when sin entered the world in the Garden of Eden not only was Adam's relationship with God damaged but also his relationship with others, himself and all creation (as evidenced clearly in the nature of the curse). And therefore, so too would Christ's kingdom of shalom manifest itself in the restoration of each of these dynamics. Francis rejected the increasingly popular and pervasive gnosticism of his age, which had begun to redefine salvation as a purely "spiritual" work of preparing our disembodied spirits for an afterlife in the clouds. Instead, he saw all of creation through the sacramental lens of the present and future kingdom of God.

To view St. Francis as an environmentalist is to miss the point, though he is certainly well-positioned as creation's patron saint. His love for creation is inseparably linked to his commitment to peace, and his radical generosity to and fraternity with the poor. Francis was enraptured by the image of the kingdom of God that was bringing the all-encompassing shalom that we are called to cocreate as the community of the Beatitudes. *Blessed are the peacemakers.* In this way, when we pray these lines we are declaring our commitment to the gospel of hope that is both immediate and future, concerned with both justice for all and our ultimate justification. They are indivisibly one in the singular, perfect will of God to which we uncompromisingly submit. That is a tall order.

In this way the first half of the Disciple's Prayer is a declaration of all that proceeded it. The prayer—all prayer, by necessity— must begin with our uncompromising submission to our God. Motivated by love and through his grace, we seek to embody his truth by becoming the community of the Beatitudes, where we are transformed into true daughters and sons of our Father King, dedicated to bringing about his kingdom, here and now. We declare our repentant dependence on him to accomplish this because we are all too often drawn away by our sinful hearts, embracing empty and false righteousness. Thus we are called daily to the cross to divest ourselves of our own wills and agendas, consecrating ourselves instead to his kingdom and his will.

It is critical that this be the foundation of all prayer, for indeed we do not pray for our own sakes or because God is somehow ignorant of our needs. The absolutely selfless devotion to God must be the starting point for all prayer, as it is for all life and faith. Only then can we dare to approach God with our needs. It is the recognition and acceptance that our obedience must not be contingent on our circumstances but entirely on our faithfulness to God and his purposes. And we don't have to fear that he will somehow miss our needs, for he is unquestionably our loving Father, who gives only good gifts to his children. Only in the abandonment of our own will and self-preservation can we truly encounter the radical grace and love of God, which is demonstrated in the rest of the Disciple's Prayer.

It can be easy for us at Little Flowers to presume that, given the gravity of the poverty and brokenness in our community, it is appropriate for us to approach him first with our needs. It is too easy for us to assume that, because of the nature of who makes up our community, he might require less of us than others, at least until we have things together. However, the first half of the Disciple's Prayer demonstrates that God is no respecter of persons. The requirements of faithfulness are absolute for every person. This doesn't ignore the need for appropriate discipleship and maturity, but rather affirms that the heart of every disciple must be fully given to God for his kingdom and his will. This is, perhaps, the greatest hurdle of faith for many, and perhaps why we have all too often tended to downplay its significance in modern evangelism.

BREAKING BREAD TOGETHER

Celebration is an important part of who we are at Little Flowers Community, so when we found out that Jimmy had had his birthday during the previous week, we decided to celebrate it with him at our Sunday gathering. Having been homeless for so long, he hadn't had a real birthday party in some time, and he was genuinely touched that we wanted to do this for him. Getting him a cake and having fun with him was not much of a sacrifice for us, but Jimmy was thrilled. He immediately headed for the door. When he returned, he was carrying several heavy grocery bags full of food and promptly took over the kitchen. If there was going to be a party in his honor, he was going to contribute to the potluck. With great pride he announced that he would be making his famous "Poor Man's Soup."

This so-called Poor Man's Soup, a dish, he said, that he made for his homeless friends whenever he could, turned out to be two huge pots full of the meatiest stews I had ever seen. Clearly Jimmy had spent a fair amount of money to make this dish special for everyone, money he could hardly afford to spend. Yet it was the very fact that he had lived with so little for so long that spurred him on to this indulgent generosity. As he slaved over the stove, he timidly asked my wife, Kim, if he could invite a few friends over. Assured that it would be great to invite them, he hopped on my laptop and sent out a few e-mails to some of his buddies (assuring them that, while we were Christians, we weren't the "freaky cult types").

That evening, the oddest assortment of people you could imagine sat around in our back yard, feasting on Poor Man's Soup and store-bought chocolate cake. It was a kingdom celebration, f-bombs and all! And in the end there was so much soup that we had several containers left over. Though we packed it up for Jimmy to take with him, he insisted that we keep most of it for ourselves. Again, we were humbled by his generosity and sense of community. He knew what it meant to not know where his "daily bread" would come from, and yet he responded with generosity instead of selfishness. We learned a great deal from Jimmy that day.

GIVE US TODAY OUR DAILY BREAD

Surprisingly, the line "give us today our daily bread" (v. 11) in the Disciple's Prayer has been one of the most problematic for Bible translators, in no small part due to the Greek word that is commonly translated as "daily." The word *epiousios* appears to be used only once in Scripture, here in this text. Not only is it only used once, but it appears that it was not used in any other known Greek text or record of common speech. Because translators rely on the wider use of a word to best understand its meaning, much debate has surrounded the meaning of its use here.[2] However, the provision of bread (the basic staple of food) by God from day to day would have most certainly reminded Jesus' followers of the miraculous provision of daily manna to the people of God as they made their exodus out of captivity in Egypt and into their Promised Land.

When Moses was leading the children of God across the wilderness toward the Promised Land, the manna that God provided only lasted a day. This meant that they were to only take what they needed for that day, trusting that God would provide what they needed the next day and the day after that. Regardless of their motivation—whether it was fear of starvation or seeing an opportunity to profit—any manna that was kept beyond one day spoiled. But the people listening to Jesus' words no longer collected manna; they already resided in the Promised Land and had their own means (meager though they might have been). In other words, they were providing for themselves, no longer relying on God's miraculous provision. They worked for what they had. They had earned it.

However, in linking their present situations with the manna of the exodus, Jesus shatters their illusions of self-reliance (and the accompanying entitlement). He reminds them that every bit of good provision, regardless of whether it was received through miraculous provision or through personal labor, is the gracious provision of God. That is why we pray, "give *us* this day *our* daily bread," for God's provision is to all his people, not simply to individuals. While not ignoring or excusing the extremes of apathy and greed, Jesus powerfully liberates us from the shame of poverty and the pride of wealth, for all that *we* have is from God for *all of us*. After all, we are now bound together in a familial loyalty that surpasses any other. This radically challenged Jesus' followers. And in this age of individualism and consumerism, it stands as a prophetic rebuke to the all too common compromises in our lives as Western Christians.

I cannot help but think of the miracle of the loaves and fishes, where Jesus feeds the multitudes with a few scraps of bread and fish, leaving more leftovers than what they had begun with. I genuinely believe that these accounts are proclaiming a supernatural event that cannot be explained by natural means. God's loving provision, like manna, can and does transcend impossible circumstances. However, some suggest that instead of a miracle of this nature, the miracle was that the hearts of the people were moved by the generosity of the meager gift and so they began to contribute what little they had hidden among them, resulting in the surplus left over after everyone had been fed. While I do not believe this was what happened, we can still glean an important truth from this interpretation of events as well. When the kingdom breaks forth into our lives, the boundaries of rights and ownership fade in the light of our unity in Christ. God's provision of daily bread is not something, then, that we experience as individual believers or small family units, but rather as an outpouring of our becoming a genuinely united community together.

This understanding is affirmed and developed further as we

look ahead to the rest of Matthew 6, as the second half of the Disciple's Prayer is a foreshadowing of the rest of Christ's message. The connection to manna is reinforced, with Jesus this time citing specific misguiding motivations—namely, selfishness—that violate the implicit commitment made with this petition. While we will explore these in more detail in the next chapters, for now let me say that Jesus clearly cautions his followers from storing up God's provision, regardless of whether it's motivated by greed and ambition or fear of deprivation. Both result in the same things: failure to fully trust in God as provider, and a limiting of our ability and willingness to share his provision with those in need.

Finally, the affirmation of *daily* bread is a reminder to us that this is a prayer we must offer continually. It is not enough to pray it once or even infrequently; the heart of this prayer must be guiding and transforming us each and every day. It is all too easy for us to make these things spiritual acts of devotion designated for specific times and places, but Jesus calls us to make this the guiding reality of every aspect of our lives. And just as we must not store up for some future need (or desire), neither can we withhold our common provision from those in need for some future day. God is calling us to give to those in need here and now, regardless of our circumstances. Again, he is no respecter of persons. Thankfully, by his miraculous provision and in the security of his unified body, the community of faith, we can be freed from the uncertainty and fear that cause us to hesitate and withhold our obedience to God and tangible love for one another.

FORGIVE US OUR DEBTS,
AS WE FORGIVE OUR DEBTORS

Jesus continues, "Forgive us our debts, as we also have forgiven our debtors" (v. 12).

Early in our ministry in our neighborhood, I made a point to ask different people in the community their impressions of Christians and the church in general. Most were respectful, but there was also an underlying hesitation, as though they weren't telling the whole story. When I encouraged them to go further, a pattern began to emerge in their answers. Most of the people I spoke to had a hard time with how we Christians focus on sin: "There are so many rules about what's wrong or evil that it feels like we can't do anything without screwing up somehow. Besides, sometimes it doesn't feel like we have a choice—we *have* to do bad stuff to survive. It's all well and good to tell me that stealing things is wrong, but I have to feed my kids somehow."

In other words, though the church might have great intentions, it is largely irrelevant in the face of their real challenges. All the food and support the church extended to them was deeply appreciated, but it did not solve the underlying challenges that created the need in the first place. They had put their fingers on a problem that has long plagued the church, summed up powerfully by the late Brazilian archbishop Dom Helder Camara when he said, "When I feed the poor, they call me a saint, but when I ask why the poor are hungry, they call me a communist."[3] Try as we might, we cannot separate the spiritual needs from the material needs.

When comparing the Disciple's Prayer in Matthew with the one found in Luke 11:1-4, we immediately see this tension in this line of the prayer. Where the Gospel of Luke reads "sins" and "everyone who sins against us," Matthew uses "debts" and "debtors." Here is another example of how the two Gospel accounts shape and inform each other, revealing the depth of Jesus' teaching. Though some would suggest that Luke clarifies what Matthew meant—that is, that it is about forgiveness of sin, not monetary or legal debt—this misses the layered meaning of how we are being called to live in this prayer. In fact, in all three Syriac versions of this text, Jesus uses the Aramaic word *khoba*, which means both material debt and sin.[4]

Without question Jesus is also referring to the forgiveness of sin, as Luke's text reveals. The statement is first and foremost a declaration of our absolute dependence on God's grace and forgiveness, daily and ultimately. Further, it is a reminder that our forgiveness is entirely undeserved, extended to us before (or whether) we asked for it. Therefore, for us to expect the gracious forgiveness of God while holding back forgiveness from others is absolutely unacceptable to God. Jesus goes so far as to say that forgiveness for our own sins is contingent on our extending entirely undeserved forgiveness to those who have wronged us, before (or whether) they asked for it (Matthew 6:14-15). We are only able to forgive because Christ's forgiveness extends through us. Just as he is the light of the world, like a blazing sun, we are the light of the world, reflecting his light into the darkness like a full moon. And because it is *his* forgiveness, it is not ours to withhold.

However, Jesus uses the language of debt intentionally, so we must pay particular attention to the greater depth of meaning. First, it should be noted that this commitment to forgive those who are indebted to us comes directly after the commitment to trust God with the communal provision he gives us. After all, it is one thing to share what we have with those in need, but it is another matter entirely to forgive a debt that is rightfully owed to us. Yet this is precisely what Jesus is suggesting, that the unparalleled grace that forgives our sin provides us with a radical model for gracious and selfless living. If all we have is God's provision, then it is up to him how to manage these debts, and he chooses forgiveness. As I have said earlier, Jesus is not setting up a new law on how to deal with debts but is calling us to a costly way of life through a heart transformed by his grace.

Second, Jesus knew how all-consuming financial debt was for people. While debt is bad enough today, in his time debt could land a person in indentured servitude or even prison. When people became slaves to debt, they forfeited their freedom and will. In other words, the bondage of sin (as well as the bondage of material debt) limits our ability to be faithful and submitted servants of God. This clearly foreshadows Jesus' later warning that we cannot serve both God and Mammon (Money). While most of us acknowledge this truth in respect to sin, our culture has us largely ignoring the dangers of becoming enslaved to material debt. Jesus is calling his people—he is *commanding* us—to live counterculturally. To do otherwise in this respect is not only an act of disobedience but an active step into the very bondage that robs us of our freedom to live obediently. To forgive people their debts also frees them to live with that same singled-minded devotion to God, which would otherwise be compromised.

When Jesus says, "For if you forgive men when they sin against you, your heavenly Father will also forgive you. But if you do not forgive men their sins, your Father will not forgive your sins" (Matthew 6:14-15), he is not offering us a transaction, a conditional forgiveness. Rather, he is making something very clear about the nature of true repentance and grace. The truly repentant understand the radical nature of God's grace and their own undeserving nature. Knowing this, how then could we refuse to extend to others what was given to us so freely? In other words, when we refuse to extend forgiveness to others, our own supposed repentance comes into question. Freely we have received, so freely we will offer forgiveness of sin and give out of God's gracious provision.

Jesus goes on to make another perplexing commitment in the prayer: "And lead us not into temptation, but deliver us from the evil one" (v. 13), which marks the end of the prayer. It is at this point that some manuscripts insert the closing affirmation: "For yours is the kingdom and the power and the glory forever. Amen" (which we will discuss shortly). However, many early manuscripts do not have this closing, moving instead into Jesus' statement in Matthew 6:14 about forgiveness being contingent on forgiving others. This always struck me as odd, as though Jesus is backtracking and stating an afterthought on forgiving our debtors. However, it occurred to me that perhaps Jesus is making a single thought, that the call for deliverance from temptation and the evil one was directly connected to the commitment to forgiveness.

The fact that Jesus refers to money more than almost any other topic tells us something about his insight into the human heart. We are selfish. Whether through greed and ambition or fearful self-preservation, it is all too easy for us to downplay or rational-ize our way out of the commitment to share with each other our "daily bread" and to truly "forgive our debtors." The rich and the poor alike are adept at sacrificing as little as possible, and Jesus knew this, which is why he taught us to pray against such tempta-tions. He also made perfectly clear where failure to resist these temptations would land us: into the hands of the evil one, the enemy. We pray this not because Jesus might lead us into tempta-tion and therefore we must convince him not to, but rather as a declaration of our discipleship, of following him. The only way to avoid the snares of the enemy is to follow without deviation the path laid out by Christ. And just as his daily bread for us is often provided through others, so too does his deliverance come through the accountability and support of the community of the crucified.

THE KINGDOM, THE POWER AND THE GLORY

While on furlough to Canada, a family of Christian ministry workers who were serving in Asia began to join us for our Little Flowers gatherings. Their teenagers commented that being with us reminded them of the house church they were a part of on the field, which we took as a great compliment. On one of the Sundays they were with us, we were discussing the last part of the Disci-ple's Prayer: "For yours is the kingdom and the power and the glory forever. Amen." As we were discussing it, Tabitha, the mother of the family, made an important point. The fact that Jesus had just warned about avoiding temptation made her realize that this closing affirmation is again a reminder that it is not about us, about our ministry accomplishments or our spiritual maturity. It is about *his* kingdom, it is by *his* power, and above all, it is for *his* glory. I was deeply struck by this reminder, something I had missed by again reading these closing words as just ritual praise.

The closing words of the Disciple's Prayer may not appear in all manuscripts, but they are well worth including and considering. Seemingly a rewording of the declaration found in 1 Chronicles 29:11-13, the closing here is consistent with the way many Jewish people would close their prayers, with declarations of praise to God. In a beautiful way, these words echo the affirmations of the first part of the prayer—beginning and ending with a declaration of God's goodness and greatness, affirming the centrality of his kingdom and his will over all things. They are declarations of eschatological hope. Though we struggle here and now, God's kingdom *will* come in its fullness. Though we are weak and suffering now, God's power *will* prevail against all evil. And though his name is misused, abused and derided (sometimes by his own people), God ultimately *will* be glorified before all of creation. It is with this hope that we can continue to faithfully follow him in building his costly kingdom.

More than that, declaring God's kingdom, power and glory was a direct affront to the Roman emperor. The language of kingdom, power and glory were to be used for the self-proclaimed god-king of the empire. So not only was this an absolute declaration of devotion to God, it was also a renunciation, even a subversive rejection, of the authority of the world. Such subversion would be a costly thing for the Jewish and early Christian believers—it was part of what cost Jesus his own life—but it was a necessary commitment to the true King and his kingdom. So too are we called to denounce the authority of the empires of this world that demand our allegiance—be it individualism, materialism, nationalism or something else. We are not to be subversive for its own sake, but rather our subversion is a byproduct of obediently following Jesus Christ as the one and only Lord and King, to whom we swear our absolute allegiance.

As our community wrestled with the implications of the Disciple's Prayer, I listened to each member's insights, questions, fears and passions. From this, we put into words how this Disciple's Prayer might sound coming from our hearts and life together as his kingdom citizens in our neighborhood:

> Father God, who unites us together as one body, one family,
> sister and brother.
> May your name be made holy by your Word and by the
> witness of us, your people.
> May your kingdom be established here and now, in and
> through us.
> May your will be our first and most immediate priority, just
> as it is to the angels above.
> Provide for us all and only what we need for life together
> and obedience to you.
> Let the gift of your undeserved grace for us overflow from
> us onto those who have wronged us, where everything
> that is owed is fully forgiven.
> Lead us on your path, away from the empty promises of our
> selfish temptations.
> Rescue us from every scheme of sin and darkness which
> would take us from that path.
> For you are King, this is your kingdom and we are your
> citizens and servants.
> All we are, all we have and all we will do is by your power
> and for your glory alone,
> in the past, in the present and in the future.
> Amen

A Confident Kingdom

Matthew 6:19-34

One afternoon a few summers ago, Kim and I were returning to the house after an afternoon out. When we were less than a block from home, we spotted two boys who we know from the neighborhood. Both were regulars at our after-school program, and we saw them frequently at the community center that shares a back lane with our house. They were walking down the sidewalk pushing a lawn mower. At each yard they would look over the fence, then move on to the next.

"Good for them," I commented. "They're trying to make some money by mowing people's lawns." We were surprised at this. They were nice enough kids, but they had a bit of a well-earned reputation in the neighborhood for being troublemakers with sticky fingers, if you know what I mean. I was encouraged by this apparent change in them and thought to myself, *Maybe they are growing up after all.*

As we moved past them, I glanced over again, hoping to catch their eye and give them an encouraging smile or thumbs up, but they were looking away and did not see me. However, when I looked over, I noticed that their lawn mower was almost exactly the same as the new electric mower we had just purchased the week before. Then it hit me. It was not *almost* the same. It *was* the same. In fact, it was my own brand new lawn mower, and they had stolen it! I quickly drove the rest of the block to our house, parked the van and confirmed the theft. Then I sprinted up the street to reclaim my mower from the rather sheepish boys, who were caught red-handed. I let them go without anything more than a mild scolding, but went home and immediately secured the mower to the back deck with a bike lock.

Living in our community, theft and vandalism are a reality of everyday life. We've had vehicles damaged, broken into and even stolen. Rakes and garden hoses, shovels and dog toys have all disappeared. The community house was even broken into once over Christmas, with some of our housemates losing a lot of property. While we learned to take precautions, we also realized that we could drive ourselves crazy worrying about our stuff and alienate our neighbors through an unintentional posture of mistrust. We have all had to learn that the Lord gives and the Lord takes away. Painful as it sometimes is, we are learning to face these realities with a somewhat strained, "Blessed be the name of the Lord!"

TREASURES IN HEAVEN

As I mentioned earlier, the second half of Jesus' teaching on the Disciple's Prayer seems to foreshadow the rest of the Sermon on the Mount. Therefore it is of little surprise that Jesus begins to talk about what living the prayer actually looks like. And he leaves little wiggle room in the radical nature of the obedience he is calling us to embrace. Few teachings could be more contentious and controversial, especially in the consumer-driven culture that is increasingly shaping the world (largely through Western economic and political powers). Here we face one of the most difficult parts of Jesus' admonitions, his teaching on money and material wealth.

> Do not store up for yourselves treasures on earth, where moth and rust destroy, and where thieves break in and steal. But store up for yourselves treasures in heaven, where moth and rust do not destroy, and where thieves do not break in and steal. For where your treasure is, there your heart will be also. (Matthew 6:19-21)

One of the more unusual (perhaps extreme) rules that Francis required of himself and his fellow friars was that they were never to touch money, even if it was given to them out of the most pious generosity. Once, when one of the brothers touched a bag of coins while simply moving it to another place, Francis rebuked him and ordered him to remove the bag of coins with his mouth and deposit it where it belonged—on the dung pile in the stables. While Francis's response to money was more extreme than necessary, it highlights how his aversion to external contaminants, such as leprosy, had been replaced by a repulsion to internal contaminants, such as greed. Having come from a place of such corrupted opulence and wealth, it is little wonder that he responded with such an extreme. Francis knew all too well how easily such wealth can twist and distort a person's heart.

Growing up, I remember first hearing the story of the rich young man who asked Jesus what he needed to do to be saved. Jesus told him to sell all that he had, give it to the poor and follow him. Shocked, I asked an adult in the church if that means we have to do the same thing. I remember their answer clearly: "No, Jamie. Jesus knew that the young man was not willing to sell all he had. As long as you are willing to give up what you have, then you are not a slave to it." While there was wisdom in this idea—for I do not believe Jesus calls all of us to sell all that we have and give it to the poor (at least not in the way that it might initially sound)— I was never satisfied with this answer. It always felt somehow compromised. After all, Jesus didn't call us to be *willing to* take up our crosses daily. He didn't ask us to be *willing to* die to ourselves. True willingness is inseparably linked to our will, our capacity to choose and act accordingly.

It would also be a mistake to assume that Jesus' teaching in this part of the Sermon on the Mount was simply a short bit of wisdom on money management or even a warning about greed and materialism. These themes are unquestionably a part of what Jesus was trying to communicate, but they are not the central emphasis. When we pull this teaching out of the larger context of the Sermon on the Mount, it is understandable why we might make those assumptions. However, its place within the wider teaching—both what came before and what follows—suggests that it's of far greater significance. It is critical that we understand this before attempting to understand his words in order to avoid the risk of either trivializing or legalizing the truths therein.

In the previous section, Jesus warned us about trying to gain recognition by our care for the poor, our pious prayers and our self-righteous fasting. He goes on here to warn against storing up for ourselves treasures on earth. However, his teaching on money stands apart as quite distinct from the previous three themes. In each of the previous topics Jesus warned against the dangers of practicing these disciplines with a wrong heart and then pointed to how they can be practiced in ways that honor God. With money, Jesus warns against the dangers of storing up treasures on earth, but this time he does *not* offer a correct way to store up material wealth. In fact, he goes on to say that money all too easily becomes a master who competes for our allegiance with God (Matthew 6:24), a competition God will not accept.

It is important to note that Jesus was not calling his people to voluntary poverty, at least not the absolute rejection of all material wealth. In reading the whole of Scripture, we can see that God clearly teaches principles for wise and faithful management of the material gifts he gives us. Rather, Jesus brings money into this part of his teaching because he knows how easily and universally we are distracted and derailed by such issues. In Luke's Sermon on the Plain, Jesus cites the parable of the rich fool to illustrate his point. In this story we find a wealthy man who, in the face of a surplus crop, decides by himself that he will store up the excess for the future. As a result, God rebukes him as a fool, telling him that his life would be taken that very night, leaving his stored-up wealth behind.

Luke's parable is a key to understanding the parallel teaching on wealth in Matthew 6. Most immediately clear to most of us is Jesus' warning about selfishness and greed. The wastefulness of storing up God's provision for us is reflected in the warning about "moth and rust" that will destroy it; this would have reminded his listeners again about the rot that consumed manna stored up by the Israelites in the wilderness. The pursuit of material wealth is incompatible with the life Christ calls us to. We must be single-minded in our pursuit of his kingdom and his righteousness. This does not make material wealth itself evil; the condition and intentions of our hearts with respect to that wealth reveal whether it masters us. In an age of rampant consumerism and materialism, Christian communities must be vigilant to this ever-present danger. Stanley Hauerwas cautions us:

> To be rich and a disciple of Jesus is to have a problem. Christians have often tried to deal with this problem by suggesting that it is not what we possess that is the problem but our attitude toward what we posses that is the problem. Some recommend, for example, that we learn to possess what we possess as if it is not really ours. This means we must always be ready to give out of our abundance or even be ready to lose all that we have. Christians, particularly in capitalist social orders, are told that it is not wealth or power that is the problem, but rather we must be good stewards of our wealth and power.[1]

However, this often results in divided loyalties and compromise. Wealth and its accumulation demand of us something we are called to give to Christ alone. Such focus often leads to the further marginalization, if not exploitation, of the poor. Hauerwas concludes: "That capitalism is an economic system justified by the production of wealth is therefore not necessarily good news for Christians."[2] This is why Jesus modeled and beckoned us into lives of simplicity and radical trust. History has demonstrated time and again that those who've had the least for Christ's sake still seemed to embrace others in love, generosity and hospitality. God's kingdom seems to most fruitfully bloom in Christian communities on the margin.

TUNNEL VISION

Jesus continues,

> The eye is the lamp of the body. If your eyes are good, your whole body will be full of light. But if your eyes are bad, your whole body will be full of darkness. If then the light within you is darkness, how great is that darkness!
>
> No one can serve two masters. Either he will hate the one and love the other, or he will be devoted to the one and despise the other. You cannot serve both God and Money. (Matthew 6:22-24)

John and Delia Knight are two of my closest friends and founding members of our Little Flowers Community. Their son, Brenden, lives with us in the community house and is part of our YWAM staff. Both John and Delia are blind. Both, however, have adapted to the challenges and live full and fulfilled lives. In fact, John has such a clear mental image of our city that most of us call him for directions to wherever we happen to be going. Real limitations are inevitable though. These by no means reduce their value as members of the community, just as Jesus isn't suggesting in verses 22-23 that physical blindness means a person is filled with spiritual darkness. Rather, he is reminding us what happens when we lose our primary focus. In other words, when we allow our reckless devotion to Christ to wander through selfishness or fear, we inevitably lose sight of Christ—not absolutely, but significantly. And Jesus knew (demonstrated by how often he warned us about it) that money and possessions in particular distract our attention.

When I told my Aunt Marty, who lives in Arizona, that Kim and I had bought our Jack Russell terrier, Dino, and that he was obsessed with chasing squirrels, she had quite the interesting story to tell us. One of her neighbors had adopted a beautiful greyhound from the shelter, a former racing dog forced to chase fake rabbits endlessly around a track. On one of their first walks they passed the famous Horseshoe Bend of the Colorado River, with its nearly one-thousand-foot drop to the water below. When they arrived, the hound spotted a rabbit. Unfortunately, the dog was not on a leash and did what came naturally: giving chase. Right over the edge of the cliff. Miraculously, the dog managed to land, bruised and cowering, on a ledge just below the top. My aunt's neighbor uses a leash every time now.

Some might see this as a good argument for not having tunnel vision, for being aware of all factors before rushing headlong into something. I have even heard some use this logic to say, essentially, "Yes, we are to follow God without compromise, but we also have to be wise in doing it. Of course we give to those in need, but we can't put our own security in jeopardy in the process." Yet Jesus seems to be rejecting this logic. When it comes to loyalty and devotion, we can only have tunnel vision, one master, even if it appears he is leading us over a precipice. Despite how things might seem, Jesus Christ is the only Master that won't lead us headlong over the cliff of destruction. He is not suggesting that we put ourselves willingly in harm's way to make a point about our faith in

him, but we need to trust him (and his community of the crucified) through costly obedience. If Christ had held back from putting his own security in jeopardy, where would that have left us?
Like it or not, Jesus wants our uncompromising devotion to him
alone. He will provide what we need. The question is, will we
choose obedience and give him the chance to prove his faithfulness? Or will we wait for a proven assurance before stepping out
in compliance? The latter is not faith, not trust at all.

This is not to say that our salvation is lost if our devotion is not
so completely single-minded. God is far too gracious for that. But
are we to go on making half an effort simply because his grace is
sufficient? Of course not! He died for our sins, and we are meant
to join him in that death daily so that we can, together, be resurrected to his purposes, his glory and his kingdom. That resurrection affords us liberty from the slavery of greed and fear. Therefore, if we participate with Christ in this redemption and salvation,
then we are called and empowered by his Spirit through the love
of the Father to live as his body, doing his will (Romans 6).

HUNGRY AND NAKED

Without question some of Jesus' listeners were motivated by
greed. Even many of the poor, who had very little to their name,
would have been enslaved to a desire for wealth. However, most
of his listeners would have been regular people who were struggling to make ends meet, especially in the face of an often ruthless and demanding occupying empire. Even in a recession, most
of us are far more secure economically than most of the people of
Jesus' day. It might have been easy for them to hear only a rebuke
of the wealthy in his words. However, Jesus goes on to make it
clear that greed is not the only way Mammon can become our
master.

Jesus also warns against storing up material wealth out of
fear that there will not be enough later. The "thieves" who come

and steal could be literal robbers or other factors, such as economic crisis, unexpected change in family circumstances or loss of the ability to work. In the face of the unknown days ahead, we can find all kinds of justifications for building a safety net for the future. Please understand that Jesus is not saying that being wise and frugal is wrong. Neither is he suggesting that saving money in case of an uncertain future is immoral. Rather, he is calling us to not let such concerns be our primary guide when dealing with our material wealth. Most North American Christians live in conditions far better than those most of the world, and even many in their own communities, live in. We have comforts and luxuries in our lives that, strictly speaking, are not essential. If we are honest with ourselves, most of us could cut a fair amount of fat off our lifestyles without causing a crisis. And yet we still choose to withhold generosity in the name of "wise money management." We still participate in economic systems that exploit the poor because of the benefits of doing so, because we "can't afford" to pay the full market price through more ethical means.

This teaching is a powerful indictment of the Christian community in the Western world. I am not denying or underplaying the very real economic challenges so many people face. However, it does not take much digging to realize that these are often born out of a culture of excess and living beyond our means. And Christians are just as prone to participate in this excess as others. Fueled by consumerism and bolstered by individualism, we have truly become enslaved to another master. Greed and poverty are not separable, for devotion to wealth for either reason locks us into the endless feast-or-famine cycle. We cannot praise the miracle of the manna (and all that it entails) and then deny such faith in God through how we live our own lives. We either believe and trust in God or we don't. And this is where the heart of Jesus' teaching becomes clear: We cannot follow Jesus as the community of the Beatitudes while caught in the pursuit of wealth, whether by greed or by fear. Jesus' call to seek first his kingdom means unwavering, primary and exclusive devotion to one King.

Yet here Jesus reminds us why such devotion is possible, why God is worthy of our trust in the face of such uncertainty. He doesn't call us to risk suffering and loss to simply test our faith or out of some misguided ascetic self-flagellation. It does not exempt us from having to work (and work hard) for our provision. Neither does it mean we are excused from our mandate to give and share what we have. Above all, it is not a promise that we will never experience trying times when things are lean, for Christ says we will find him in and among the poor and hungry. Rather than a law to be obeyed and through which we receive an immediate, material reward, it is about the eternal fruit of obedience to the law of love and grace that is Christ.

Instead, we can trust him and live this radical obedience because he is our Father who loves us. He is the Father who loves his creation so much that he cares for the birds and flowers. How much more will he care for his children, made in his very image? We must embrace these truths as more than theological ideas; they are realities that lead us to live risky and selfless lives of unrelenting and active devotion to God. Anxiety is born out of unbelief, and unbelief becomes a seed through which our nature and actions are formed. It is the seed that chokes out the flowering beauty of trusting our loving Father to meet all our needs, liberating us from self-interest in order that we might love and serve him and others for the sake of his glory and his costly kingdom.

DON'T WORRY, BE RIGHTEOUS

It is undeniably clear in his last words in Matthew 6 that Jesus calls us to trust and follow him without concern for what tomorrow might bring. Instead of worrying, we are called to "seek first his kingdom."

Therefore I tell you, do not worry about your life, what you will eat or drink; or about your body, what you will wear. Is not life more important than food, and the body more important than clothes? Look at the birds of the air; they do not sow or reap or store away in barns, and yet your heavenly Father feeds them. Are you not much more valuable than they? Who of you by worrying can add a single hour to his life?

And why do you worry about clothes? See how the lilies of the field grow. They do not labor or spin. Yet I tell you that not even Solomon in all his splendor was dressed like one of these. If that is how God clothes the grass of the field, which is here today and tomorrow is thrown into the fire, will he not much more clothe you, O you of little faith? So do not worry, saying, "What shall we eat?" or "What shall we drink?" or "What shall we wear?" For the pagans run after all these things, and your heavenly Father knows that you need them. But seek first his kingdom and his righteousness, and all these things will be given to you as well. Therefore do not worry about tomorrow, for tomorrow will worry about itself. Each day has enough trouble of its own. (Matthew 6:25-34)

Like in the Disciple's Prayer, we are again called to make his kingdom our priority, even before our own well-being—not out of self-destructive neglect, but rather out of radical trust and obedience to our Father God who provides all that we need and gives only good gifts to his children. Further, this obedience flows out of our becoming the community of the Beatitudes, surrounded by others who care for us and help to meet our needs, as we help to meet theirs. The Disciple's Prayer, like the Beatitudes before it, gives us a glimpse into the nature of the kingdom that so beautifully reflects the nature of the King. However, Jesus does not say "seek first his kingdom and second his righteousness." He instead teaches us that together with seeking his kingdom we are also to seek his righteousness. In other words, we cannot seek God's kingdom and not seek his righteousness, and we cannot seek his righteousness without seeking his kingdom. This should immediately remind us of his indivisible command to love God and love our neighbor as ourself.

As we have already seen in detail, righteousness is better understood through the lens of justice, that is, right relationship with others, especially in respect to those on the margins, "the least of these." Again we are reminded that God's kingdom and justice transform the here and now, affecting the whole of creation, not just some imagined, spiritual segment of our being; such a division between the physical and the spiritual is foreign to Christ. Every individual and even all of creation was understood to be indivisibly whole. For example, the Old Testament word for the soul—*nefesh* in Hebrew—represents the physical body of an individual as much as the spiritual nature. This is critical for us to understand, because the righteousness/justice we are called to seek in the kingdom here and now is concerned with the whole person, the whole creation, not just a disembodied soul that needs to find security in the afterlife.

Seeking justice, then, orients our hearts and our minds toward the other, not ourselves. Our own needs are covered, so we can give ourselves completely over to doing justice, loving mercy and walking humbly with God (Micah 6:8) in the context of his kingdom. By the world's standards, it is a reckless commitment to making the needs of others more important than our own, even to the point of not protecting our interests against material poverty. Consider the implications of such devotion—what it would cost us, what it would look like. Imagine what the world would think of Christians if *this* is what most commonly characterized our faith. It has happened before; the early church, for example, formed hospices for the poor and the sick regardless of their religious devotion.

We've seen it in the lives of people like St. Clare and St. Francis of Assisi, whose foolishly reckless trust in God led them to call poverty their fair Lady, because nothing could rob them of God's provision. When we hunger and thirst for this justice, we are blessed. This is the justice for which we can expect to be persecuted. It will cost us a great deal, but it is only in seeking both his kingdom and his justice that we see what it means to be both salt and light to the world, to be the community of the Beatitudes, the community of the crucified and the community of the resurrection.

We are called to believe the gospel in our hearts and minds. We are called to proclaim the gospel in our words and deeds. We are called to live the words of Jesus at all costs and without compromise. This is what it means to seek first his kingdom and his righteousness. Then, when we do this, all the other details of life will be given to us by God. Therefore, we must crucify any worry that robs us of our single-minded devotion to Christ.

This isn't something that can be achieved, but by his grace and his Spirit it is a shared way of life to be pursued more and more each day. Little Flowers Community has not "arrived" at this high ideal, but rather we devote ourselves to living with such faith one day at a time. Our inner-city community was not completely transformed overnight or even in the few years we have lived and served here. However, through God's faithfulness to us, our obedience has contributed to his kingdom breaking forth little by little in the neighborhood. Such a commitment is difficult and demanding. However, Jesus would not call us to a lifestyle that is impossible for us to follow. Seek first his kingdom and justice, and he will provide us with all else that we need.

From Judgment to Humility

Matthew 7:1-12

There are some biblical scholars who suggest that the last section of the Sermon on the Mount (Matthew 7) doesn't fit naturally into the flow of the larger message. Some simply chalk it up to Matthew's attempt to bring in some other teachings of Jesus that he felt were important but which ultimately do not follow the pattern of the rest of the text. However, if we pay close attention to the threads running through the entire Sermon, this chapter is not only a natural conclusion but an essential part of the greater whole.

In Matthew 5 we are introduced to the radical nature of the Christian life and being transformed into the people of the Beatitudes. In chapter 6 Jesus goes on to describe the nature of true righteousness and justice, humble, hidden and glorifying to God. What is described is powerful and extraordinary. Those who follow Christ in this way are promised God's blessing and his kingdom. It is inevitable, then, that Jesus would go on to teach how his disciples should relate to one another. And what more common challenge do we face than our impulse to judge each other?

Thus Jesus teaches, "Do not judge, or you too will be judged. For in the same way you judge others, you will be judged, and with the measure you use, it will be measured to you" (Matthew 7:1-2).

Imagine what it would have been like for the disciples and the crowds listening to Jesus' words. To be invited to participate in such an extraordinary, though costly, kingdom would have stirred a great deal of passion among them. As Matthew 7:28-29 indicates, Jesus taught with greater authority than the other religious elites. Not only did he make true righteousness achievable (by grace) for every person, but he also promised the liberty of messianic fulfillment that could not be touched by the most powerful occupying military force in the world. The temptation to seize such promises as fodder for vindication and judgment would be all too clear. Take *that*, you self-righteous teachers of the law! In your face, you bullying Roman imperialists!

Jesus knew all too well that his followers (then and now) would need to be reminded that such attitudes were not only unacceptable but dangerous: "For in the same way you judge others, you will be judged, and with the measure you use, it will be measured to you" (v. 2). Christians are often seen as especially judgmental, which is an accusation that is difficult to defend against. Jesus saw this arrogant and self-serving propensity and explicitly addresses it here.

What does Jesus mean, though, when he warns us not to judge others? Surely he is not asking us to deny our critical skills of discernment. After all, through his teaching, both in the Sermon on the Mount and elsewhere, Jesus requires that we use our discernment to judge between that which is good and that which is not. Jesus is by no means teaching that we are to ignore what people say and do to each other, as though it is none of our business. Far from it. Rather, Jesus is specifically addressing the nature of our hearts in the face of other people's sin: condemnation. And he does so quite creatively.

BLINDED HEALERS

Recently, while out doing some daily errands, Delia had something of an interesting encounter with a fellow shopper. While partially sighted, Delia is legally blind, which makes many everyday tasks that many of us take for granted far more difficult. Equipped with her dark shades and white cane, she set forth to do her weekly shopping. During that particular trip to the store, Delia was interrupted by the gravelly voice of an elderly woman, who clearly had spent a lifetime as a smoker. Exasperated, the woman loudly declared: "Can you please help me? I can't see a dang thing!"

At first Delia was taken aback, glancing around to see who she had spoken to. Was this woman talking to her? Surely her eyesight couldn't be any worse than her own, so what did she think Delia could do to help her? However, when a nearby store employee responded, she realized that she had not been the focus of this request for help. With a silent chuckle to herself, Delia imagined the comical potential if that particular scenario had been played out. She recounted this little incident to me on the phone while we were talking about this part of Jesus' teaching. Delia realized that her own blindness made her ability to help this other woman nearly impossible. She commented to me that she was tempted to sidle up to the lady and say, "I hear ya, sister! I can't see a dang thing either," but she resisted the temptation. In that moment, though she was unable to help the woman, Delia was able to identify with her. The woman's public confession of her need allowed Delia to recognize and be real about her own needs.

This story highlights the critical starting point of Jesus' teaching, giving us an insight into his call for us to resist our impulse to judge others.

> Why do you look at the speck of sawdust in your brother's eye and pay no attention to the plank in your own eye? How can you say to your brother, "Let me take the speck out of your eye," when all the time there is a plank in your own

eye? You hypocrite, first take the plank out of your own eye, and then you will see clearly to remove the speck from your brother's eye. (Matthew 7:3-5)

Jesus is clearly pointing out that, even as Christians, we will suffer the limitations of our sinful nature. Any righteousness that we have is not by our own merit or effort, but reflected from Christ alone. We are as dependent on God's grace as the brother with the "speck" in his eye. This sense of mutual sinfulness and common dependence on God must be the starting place of our relationship with others, both within the community of faith and in the wider world. This identification with the other, the humble recognition that we have not fully arrived at perfection, reveals that only One is qualified to cast judgment, and he chooses grace.

However, Jesus does not stop there. He isn't saying, "You're all pretty screwed up, so don't point out each other's weaknesses. Just deal with your own sin—in other words, mind your own business." Rather, Jesus goes on to say, "First take the plank out of your own eye, and then you will see clearly to remove the speck from your brother's eye" (v. 5). Clearly Jesus *does* call us to aid our brothers and sisters in removing the speck of sin from their eyes, but the posture has changed radically. First, only in seeing the sinfulness in ourselves, and then working to overcome that hindrance, are we able to effectively see the challenges of others clearly enough to help them. Second, when we acknowledge and experience the painful and difficult process of having such sin addressed in ourselves, our hearts are shaped by the understanding and compassion necessary to do so appropriately with others. Few places exemplify this kind of mutuality and accountability like many twelve-step programs, such as Alcoholics Anonymous. The truest transformation comes when we share in the healing grace of God together in light of our common brokenness and mutual dependence.

In our culture of individualism, though, it is easy to read Jesus' words as suggesting that we all must fix ourselves before helping others. This is impossible, as the analogy of the plank and speck demonstrates. After all, if we are to help our sister and brother remove the speck from their eye, it stands to reason that we are also dependent on our sisters and brothers to help us remove the plank from our own eye. Therefore, the humble mutuality in serving one another in our shared brokenness is further established. This is where the discipline of confession emerges in all its difficult beauty. Stanley Hauerwas writes:

> The disciples are not to judge because any judgment that needs to be made has been made. For those who follow Jesus to act as if they can, on their own, determine what is good and what is evil is to betray the work of Christ. Therefore, the appropriate stance for the acknowledgement of evil is the confession of sin. We quite literally cannot see clearly unless we have been trained to see "the log that is in [our] eye." But it is not possible for us to see what is in our eye because the eye cannot see itself. That is why we are able to see ourselves only through the vision made possible by Jesus—a vision made possible by our participation in a community of forgiveness that allows us to name our sins.[1]

As we passionately seek to live out the radical ideals of what it means to be followers of Jesus, that very zeal can all too easily become a self-righteousness that leads to judging others. This admonition to remain humble and dependent on God and his people helps us resist that self-serving tendency. The beauty of God's redemptive grace, however, transforms this very experience. Rather than it being a constant reminder of how horrible and sinful we are, which then keeps us too cowed to judge others, Jesus powerfully uses the very process of confession and repentance to help others discover the hope and liberty in his grace.

This was illustrated powerfully when someone very close to me confessed long-term marital unfaithfulness to their spouse. This person faithfully sought forgiveness and healing, and the family has emerged stronger than ever, a beautiful witness to the power of God's work. The willingness to openly confess and do the work of repentance and reconciliation has transformed a tragic event into an example of loving faithfulness we all learned from. Further, this humble repentance and commitment to reconciliation stands as an example to all of us, who, whenever we sin, demonstrate the same devastating unfaithfulness to our one and true Bridegroom, Jesus Christ, pointing toward the beautiful and redemptive hope in his forgiveness.

Confession of sin is not easy, and the process itself can become twisted by our sinful nature. However, learning the discipline of being a confessing community will not only minimize the risk of becoming self-righteous judges, but create a context in which people can find the genuine hope of healing and forgiveness in light of their very real brokenness and sin. Judgment seeks to achieve community purity by exclusion, while grace seeks true purity through confession and redemption. It is perhaps one of the most powerful living proclamations of the good news of Jesus Christ to a waiting and watching world, but only if we are willing to humbly live it out each day.

OF DOGS AND SWINE

As Jesus called his followers to this absolute commitment to humility and grace, there can be little doubt that many of them (and us) began to consider the implications of such radical redemption. Surely there are those who deserve our judgment. Surely there are those whose rejection and scorn of truth and love has earned them our most unequivocal indictment. Jesus taught that rather than judging people, we are to extend to them what we ourselves have received—that is, the undeserved grace of the gospel, both actively proclaimed and demonstrated by his people to a watching world. However, he was not ignorant of the reality that despite our commitment to love instead of judge, there is no guarantee that some will not reject or abuse us for it.

Even in the face of generosity, hospitality, love, peace and grace, there will be people who will not accept the grace we extend to them, and will even openly mock and scorn it. It is to these people that Jesus is referring when he immediately goes on to say: "Do not give dogs what is sacred; do not throw your pearls to pigs. If you do, they may trample them under their feet, and then turn and tear you to pieces" (Matthew 7:6).

By judging some as dogs and swine, it seems Jesus is committing the very sin he has just cautioned against, but closer inspection proves something far different. He does not tell us to attempt to aggressively force his grace on those who completely reject it, but rather that we should move on. Here we see the practical implications of his judgment on Sodom and Gomorrah (Matthew 10:15); this was practiced by Paul throughout his ministry (Acts 13:44-51; 18:5-6; 28:17-28). Jesus is not blind to the harshest rejection and abuse that some will dish out to his people, but still he calls us to withhold judgment and instead move on to those who are more open to receiving the love and grace of God.[2]

But in what appears to be a biting insult to those who reject the gospel, calling them dogs and swine (two of the harshest critiques among the Jews), Jesus is also cleverly turning the responsibility back upon us, his followers. He is not simply calling gospel-resistant people "dogs" and "swine" but is confronting us with our own self-righteousness. It is in our refusal to be beaten, in our unrelenting desire for vindication and in our dogged zeal to judge the blatant sinfulness of those who reject the gospel that we make the gospel worthy of dogs and pigs. In our refusal to "shake the dust from our feet" and move on, we use the gospel as a bludgeon and thus make it no more worthy than something cast before beasts. We disparage Christ, who died to give us grace, by failing to let that same grace touch even this aspect of our lives.

The teachings of Jesus in the Sermon on the Mount are not meant to be axioms and exhortations that can serve as helpful sound bites. Rather, they are a manifesto of the kingdom Jesus is cultivating. To follow these teachings, we need to first follow Christ—at all costs. Grounded in the humility and mutuality of grace, we must "spur one another on toward love and good deeds" (Hebrews 10:24). However, it is not up to us to aggressively enforce the expectations of Christ on those who are not open to the gospel. Ultimately, this ends up working against the very kingdom that we are called to embody in our words and deeds. The implications are not limited to personal application. The Sermon must touch every aspect of what it means to be Christians in community with one another, as well as a people living in but not of the world. It speaks to the question of who we trust: the people we meet each day or the systems of power (political, social, economic) that make up our societies. As one author puts it, "When Christians have entrusted the coming of the kingdom to the powers of this world, the sacred pearl has all too quickly been trampled underfoot."[3]

ASK, SEEK AND KNOCK

The great task that lies ahead should not be lost on any of us. The beautiful vision of God's kingdom we are called to live and embrace seems beyond reach, and utterly impossible for any of us to achieve. This has led many scholars to therefore proclaim that the Sermon was never meant to be obeyed. Instead, it intentionally demonstrates through its overwhelming idealism how impossible it is for us to attempt to earn salvation by works. This conclusion is understandable, for it is impossible for any of us to do what Jesus calls us to do—to be what he calls us to be—in this teaching. However, we fail to remember that Jesus also taught his disciples that "with man this is impossible, but with God all things are possible" (Matthew 19:26). This is not to say that he expects perfection, as his teaching constantly references the reality of our brokenness and failings. Rather, it is another affirmation that any good that we might do or become is but the reflected glory of God working in and through us (and sometimes, in spite of us).

It is to this impossibility that Jesus goes on to say: "Ask and it will be given to you; seek and you will find; knock and the door will be opened to you. For everyone who asks receives; he who seeks finds; and to him who knocks, the door will be opened" (Matthew 7:7-8).

Here Jesus is teaching us about prayer in a different context than in the Disciple's Prayer. This admonition is not directed toward the anxieties, expectations and needs of the previous teaching, but to the impossible task of living as Christ commands us in the Sermon on the Mount. So what are we to ask for? What must we seek? Who is behind the door that we seek to enter? The parallel teaching in the Sermon on the Plain makes this abundantly clear: "If you then, though you are evil, know how to give good gifts to your children, how much more will your Father in heaven give the Holy Spirit to those who ask him!" (Luke 11:13).

The Holy Spirit, the fullness of the all-loving, all-powerful God, dwells in us, uniting us as his body. The Spirit makes the impossible task of building his kingdom possible. Jesus' own ministry was inaugurated when the Holy Spirit descended on him. One of the last promises Jesus made to his disciples before ascending to the Father was that he would send his Spirit, and they would do even greater things than he had! And the Holy Spirit's coming at Pentecost exploded God's fledgling church into a missional force that defied circumstances and thrived in the face of persecution, suffering and even (perhaps especially) martyrdom. So we too must pursue the Spirit of God, acknowledging our inability and inadequacies, but demonstrating our faithfulness in his power, where obedience to him is the only measure of success we need concern ourselves with.

Here the contrast becomes the clearest: the self-righteous seek to establish their authority by judging others to be less worthy, while the truly faithful receive the fullness of God's power and authority by declaring themselves weak and in need—asking, seeking and knocking. And God graciously gives his Spirit to all who ask in faith—not because our prayers inform him of our need or because he needs to be coerced to do so, but rather because he is our loving Father, who wants only good for his children: "Which of you, if his son asks for bread, will give him a stone? Or if he asks for a fish, will give him a snake? If you, then, though you are evil, know how to give good gifts to your children, how much more will your Father in heaven give good gifts to those who ask him!" (Matthew 7:9-11). He does not thrust this gift on the unwilling, but waits for us, as the father waited with open arms and an open heart for his prodigal son to return. All that is required is that we return home to the loving embrace of our Father.

THE GOLDEN RULE

Jesus then utters the words that will forever be known as the golden rule: "So in everything, do to others what you would have them do to you, for this sums up the Law and the Prophets (Matthew 7:12)." Most people are more familiar with Luke's more concise version: "Do to others as you would have them do to you" (6:31). We know this admonition has existed in various forms in other religions and cultures, though usually in its negative form ("Do not do to others what you would not have them do to you"). As a stand-alone axiom, it is truly a profound and even demanding standard to live by that deserves our reflection and application. However, when Jesus said "so in everything," he was using a turn of phrase that let the Jewish listener know that he was summing up his previous thoughts in this one point.

Some people use the golden rule as a means to require better treatment from others. In other words, when they feel mistreated, they remind the offender, "Do to others as you would have them do to you." Fair enough! However, this is not the way Jesus calls his followers to obey this commandment. Especially given the previous discussion on not judging others but focusing on our own heart, it is clear that Jesus wants us to focus on our own behavior. Later in Matthew, Jesus again sums up the Law and the Prophets: "'Love the Lord your God with all your heart and with all your soul and with all your mind.' This is the first and greatest commandment. And the second is like it: 'Love your neighbor as yourself.' All the Law and the Prophets hang on these two commandments" (Matthew 22:37-40).

The phrase "love your neighbor as yourself" has always given me pause. Here, Jesus is affirming the importance of having love for myself. After all, I am created in his image, loved by him beyond measure and worth the greatest sacrifice. However, without diminishing this truth, there is another component here that we miss. Jesus is also powerfully subverting our natural (and often selfish) tendency to look out for number one. Consider the energy, time and commitment you have invested in taking care of yourself—avoiding harm, enjoying comforts and pleasure, pursuing fulfillment and overcoming problems. In one powerful statement Jesus commandeers that which occupies our greatest energy and attention—our love of self—and turns it toward the love and care of others. It is not enough to be good people who treat others with respect. Instead we are called to love others with the same commitment, sacrifice and devotion that we have for ourselves. This is what the golden rule teaches us to do.

While we aspire to this at Little Flowers, it is never easy. Aside from our natural, selfish inclinations to focus on ourselves and our own needs, many people in our community face significant daily crises, whether financial, relational, legal or any combination thereof. It is easy for us to rationalize this commitment away with the well-intentioned conviction, *Once things get better in my life I will give more of myself to others.* Jesus makes no room for this. Just as he requires our single-minded devotion to him, as we have seen so clearly throughout the Sermon, he also requires commitment to one another. Once again we see that our love for and obedience to God is inseparable from our love for and service to our neighbors, to all others. Why? Because they are unequivocally loved by God, and, empowered and transformed by his Spirit, we cannot help but love what he loves. Not simply with the blind devotion of a religious adherent but with the genuine, relational commitment that reflects a Father's love for his children.

OF SEEDS, ROOTS AND LITTLE FLOWERS

As we seek to live out Jesus' mandates as a community, it inevitably means that we are confronted with difficult situations and uncomfortable questions. By suspending judgment and instead creating a welcoming community of mutually broken people seeking God's healing and salvation together, we do away with the unofficial screening process that so often filters certain people out at the front doors of the church. This means that we find ourselves in close community with people who do not exemplify what we typically think of as good churchgoers. Inevitably, especially when the questions about what it means to be an inclusive and embracing community come up, someone is bound to ask, "OK, but where do we draw the line?"

This is where Jesus' teaching again subverts our expectations, showing us that we are asking the wrong question—or at least asking it at the wrong time and place. This does not mean that the underlying concerns of this question are not important; every healthy community requires appropriate boundaries. The question, though, is how and where and what is involved in setting those boundaries. Too often we feel we have to start with a line or with a set of ideals which people have to adhere to (or at least acknowledge) before they can meaningfully belong to the community of faith. I believe this goes against the heart of how Jesus embodied these dynamics. In our community we have a simple (if imperfect) analogy that helps us articulate what we believe God calls us to. Fittingly, it is the analogy of little flowers.

In Mark 9, when Jesus responds to the man whose son was being tormented by an evil spirit, the man declares, "I do believe; help my unbelief." Here we see a person who clearly believes in Christ and his authority to heal his son. Yet he also acknowledges that he needs to be saved from his unbelief. This is the mustard seed of faith, the tiny *seed of belief*. Understanding belief as a seed says a great deal—it is a small, simple medium containing untold promise and complexity. It holds within it the potential for something far greater than itself. A seed on its own is nothing; a seed must be planted.

We typically presume that belief plants itself in our individual hearts, and while there is an element of truth here, the best soil in which the seed of belief will sprout into new life is Christ. Like a seed, we must die to our sin-isolated selves before we can spring to new life in Christ as his body. Here is where the shift in our thinking takes place, because we are prone to look at our salvation in Christ through purely individualistic terms. Rather, Jesus has (by the Holy Spirit) made us into his body, the church. Therefore, it is in the *soil of belonging*, in the embrace of true community, that the seed of belief can best be reborn to new life. Unless that seed has the life-giving, life-sustaining soil in which to be planted, we cannot expect its transformation.

As the seed of belief sprouts new life in the soil of belonging, it begins to be shaped by the DNA inherent in the seed. It is being raised into the image of the resurrected Christ, while also being restored to its intended nature of being created in God's image. It spreads its roots in the soil of belonging and sprouts into the world as the little flower it was meant to be. As clumsy as the term might sound, these are the little *flowers of behavior.* The flower acts and grows and reproduces according to its nature (which, again, is Christ). It does not have to behave like a flower in order to belong and take root, but rather it is able to be a flower only after it has been embraced, rooted and nurtured in the context of belonging.

So where are the boundaries? Unlike seeds and flowers, our free will means that we can and do make choices that go against the intentions of God, that our behavior doesn't inevitably reflect the DNA of Christ. However, this understanding teaches us that for the new life to be born, we have to accept a degree of uncertainty when embracing people with, as of yet, unflowered belief. Jesus did not teach that we need to examine each seed before we plant it. He said we will know the nature of the seed by the nature of the fruit it produces. This demands that we allow fruit to be produced first. This is risky. This is messy. This is complicated. But this has been our commitment.

With this understanding, then, the teaching of Jesus that we explored in this chapter reminds us that our focus must be on the nature and the quality of the soil in which the seeds of belief are planted. In other words, our primary focus should not be policing who is or is not welcome in our communities, but rather we should focus on creating communities in which the fragile but promising beliefs and hopes of others have the best opportunity to be rooted and to thrive. Looking to our own hearts in an act of healthy self-love also becomes an expression of loving others, because they will benefit from our commitment to humility and repentance. This is a significant paradigm shift, moving from a posture of policing to an almost maternal care for the new life being formed in our community. We bear the greater responsibility at this stage. *Our* behavior, not the outsider's, must be held to a high standard. The Sermon on the Mount is critical in forming us into the kind of soil in which people can be fruitfully rooted.

I can't help but think of the story of the woman caught in adultery who was brought before Jesus for judgment (John 8:1-11). By
the letter of the law this woman had crossed the line. Her behavior clearly allowed for the absolute act of exclusion—death by
stoning. But Jesus does not exclude her—don't miss how critical
this is—but rather stoops down and begins to draw in the dirt.
Then he turns to the accusers, addressing the sinful behavior of
the *believers* before that of the woman caught in sin, and invites
anyone without sin to cast the first stone. Then he returns to the
dirt. When he stands up again, he sees that he and the woman are
alone. He asks her if anyone is accusing her, to which she replies
that there is no one. Then Jesus says, "Neither do I condemn you."
Notice that she has not repented or confessed her sin. And yet
Jesus, the only man who could have rightfully condemned her,
does not. Only then does he say, "Go now and leave your life of
sin." Only here, at the very end of this exchange, does Jesus address her behavior. He knows that her behavior is more likely to
be transformed by his loving defense and embrace (which put
him at very real risk) than through fear of judgment, legitimate as
it might have been.

Living in the Franciscan brotherhood might have been roman-
ticized by some (as it often is today), but their shared life of poverty would have worn that quite thin very early on. Like any community the friars were confronted with relational tensions that
would deeply and consistently try their patience and grace for one
another. And yet others saw in them an attractive and powerful
love. One early brother noted, "How great was the love that flourished in the members of this pious society! For whenever they
came together anywhere, or met one another along the way, there
a shoot of spiritual love sprang up, sprinkling over all the seed of
true affection."[4] Francis and his brothers understood what it means
to live these words of Jesus.

Where do we draw the line? Sometimes, when I read the story of

Jesus and this woman, I imagine that when Jesus stooped down he was drawing a line in the sand. He drew a line in the sand between the accusers and the woman. And he stood on her side of the line. This is the kind of community I believe we are creating at Little Flowers, and one I believe will transform the way we engage with our neighbors in the world around us. It is a vision of the community of the crucified that Christ calls us all to pursue.

Gates and Fruit

Matthew 7:13-23

Jimmy recently returned to the city for a visit, asking if he could once again crash at our place for a few days. Having not seen him in some time, we happily welcomed him in. Within minutes of his arrival, however, we knew that all was not well with him. His untreated mental illness was clearly getting worse. Convinced that he was a prophet of God with strange mystical powers, he had spent countless hours planning and recording his vision for saving the world. While his heart was clearly pointed toward something good and noble, when he let me read his manifesto, I become very concerned. His ever-changing belief system, clouded by the delusions of his illness, included randomly incorporated bits and pieces from other religions and spiritualities. Occasionally he would invite me to comment on his ideas, which I attempted to do honestly and carefully. I explained what we believed about Jesus and what that meant to us, but it soon became clear that he was not in a place where a rational explanation was going to make much of a difference. He was always gracious and never argued against what we shared, but it was as though he could not hear anything beyond the voices in his head.

While Jimmy's case is an extreme one, deeply affected by his mental health, our conversations made me realize that following Christ is a very singular and distinct way of life. Don't get me wrong. It's not as though I was unfamiliar with the unique and often exclusive claims of Christianity. After all, I was raised as an evangelical Christian, where the exclusive claims were often our shiniest badges of honor. Rather, as important as doctrinal soundness is, I began to realize that Jesus was not primarily calling us to this form of exclusivity. Jesus is primarily concerned with my living fidelity to him—loving him from a heart of such devotion that it necessarily transforms every aspect of the way I live. Following Jesus surpasses a cognitive, intellectual or even emotional conviction that an idea is true (though it is obviously a necessary component). It is, instead, a living witness of his truth proven by being his body here and now, and by my life—our lives as his people—being entirely his to command. They are!

As beautiful and exciting as this truth is, Jesus knew that such fidelity was rare. He knew that while many would be inspired by his teaching and worship him as the Messiah and King, far fewer would be willing to follow him in obedience, paying the price exacted by the cross of being his true disciples. Sadly, history seems to demonstrate how accurate this is. Even before Jesus' birth, God's people demonstrated their wavering faithfulness time and again. Since his ascension, the church has done little better. This is not to dismiss the work of God's Spirit in his people through history, but it acknowledges that Jesus' words at the end of the Sermon on the Mount are deadly true. Here we must pay very careful attention to the warnings he has for us and seek, by his grace and the power of his Spirit, to avoid the pitfalls that so easily ensnare us.

THE BROAD PATH

One of the joys of living on the banks of the beautiful Rainy River while growing up was that my family regularly participated in a truly Canadian pastime: canoeing. Throughout my teen years I would spend hours every day (weather permitting) paddling alone along the banks of the river, watching the rich diversity of birds and other wildlife, waiting for sunset or visiting with some of the patient fishing groups that were anchored all along the way. I became a very seasoned canoeist, feeling almost more comfortable in that little boat than I did on dry land.

Being an avid reader, I also loved reading about canoeing. I remember reading one story about a couple of young guys who were canoeing down the Mississippi River, from its source in Minnesota all the way to the Gulf of Mexico. They marveled at this river that began as no more than a stream and eventually opened up to become the widest river in America. As they neared the end of their journey, they found that the unseasonably high waters made it even more difficult to know where they were on the river. At one point they decided to double-check their map. As one of the men leaned over the chart, he said he was pretty sure they were near the center of the river, right on course. His friend laughed out loud and strongly disagreed, for just as he'd made that assessment, they floated within a few feet of a stop sign and a mailbox jutting out of the water. They were far beyond the boundaries of the Mississippi, floating over a flooded field near some unfortunate farmer's homestead.

In my own dreams of canoeing the Mississippi, I was less interested in those early stretches of the river, where it was at times so narrow that someone could jump across from one bank to the other. Rather, in my imagination, I longed for the broad and sweeping Mississippi of steamboats and Huck Finn. I think many people view Christianity with the same attitude—why choose the narrow banks of a religion of strict moral rules when they can enjoy the great freedom and beauty of a life full of wider possibilities? And in fairness, their criticism is well deserved, as we have all too often made following Christ nothing more than adherence to certain limiting behaviors and relationships.

This broad stream of freedom is not, however, what Jesus is calling us to in Matthew 7:13-14: "Enter through the narrow gate. For wide is the gate and broad is the road that leads to destruction, and many enter through it. But small is the gate and narrow the road that leads to life, and only a few find it." After all, life is not a leisurely vacation down a river. Our life is a gift from God, an opportunity of grace to reconcile and restore the broken relationship we have with him, each other and all of creation, by the work of Christ. The consequence of our choices is not merely finding ourselves laughably in the wrong place, but rather missing the purposes and will of God, the only truly good reward. From this perspective, then, the limitations of the narrow river banks become helpful and necessary boundaries in pursuit of our singular destination. Further, the broad, sweeping freedom of the wide, flowing river becomes the dangerous, aimless path that, lacking any firm boundaries, fails to lead us to God and therefore leads us to destruction.

Again, it is critical that we do not confuse this narrowness or these boundaries with moral policing. No matter how valid the rules or the sins we seek to avoid are, making those sins (or the prohibitions against them) the focus of what it means to follow Jesus diminishes and even disparages the radical and beautiful call of Christ to us, his disciples. The boundaries that make up the narrow way are quite clear in Jesus' teaching. The entire Sermon on the Mount lays out for us the path that Jesus calls us to follow— the path of humble repentance, the path of justice and peacemaking, the path of pure hearts and single-minded obedience, the path of faith and trust, the path of grace and selfless love, the path of mutual brokenness and redemption. It is the path of the prodigal returning to the loving embrace of the waiting Father. It is the path on which we transform our natural concern for our own well-being into the selfless love and service of others. It is, above all, the path where we actively and absolutely love and obey God with every aspect of our beings, as individuals and his united people.

In one sense the narrow path is not difficult, while in another it is very difficult. It is not difficult, for example, because following Christ is clear and simple. It is like an Olympic athlete standing on the high board of an Olympic diving pool in order to leap into the water below. The act of jumping into the water is quite simple, merely requiring one step forward and then letting gravity do the rest. Yet few of us would so easily take that step! Why? Because such a step goes against our very core and common sense for survival. We long for the end result—the cool and refreshing embrace of the water below, and the completion of the task—but we balk at the path we are asked to take in arriving there. Even when we logically understand the safety of the water below, we are hardwired to protect ourselves against all the potential and imagined risks that such a leap might bring. It is, therefore, also very difficult because it requires us to give up control in the face of those risks and all the ensuing consequences.

It is in this way that following the path of Christ is most difficult. What we are called to do, what we are called to be, is not all that complicated or complex, but it invites us into a space of great uncertainty, insecurity and risk. We long for the safety, peace and comfort that comes in Jesus Christ, yet we balk at the cost that such discipleship exacts. And just like my own first time standing on that high diving platform, we can quite easily rationalize and minimize the necessity of such an "extreme" commitment. After all, it would still be quite brave for the athlete to dive from one of the lower diving platforms. Or better yet, why not just slip into the water gently from poolside? They would end up in the same place in the end, right? Yet the very task for which the athletes find themselves on the high board would be ignored; they'd be failing to represent their country and their team. Sadly, too many of us end up making these very choices by lessening or compromising our commitments to follow Christ. Bonhoeffer noted:

> The disciple is dragged out of his relative security into a life of absolute insecurity (that is, in truth, into the absolute security and safety of the fellowship of Jesus), from a life which is observable and calculable (it is, in fact, quite incalculable) into a life where everything is unobservable and fortuitous (that is, into one which is necessary and calculable), out of the realm of finite (which is in truth infinite) into the realm of infinite possibilities (which is the one liberating reality).
> . . . It is nothing else than bondage to Jesus Christ alone, completely breaking through every programme, every ideal, every set of laws.[1]

Jesus does not give us the option to take the easier path. In fact, he gives us only two choices: we can follow him to fullness of life or we can choose to not follow him, which leads to our own demise. He makes it clear that he is calling us through this very narrow, clearly defined gate. And while we know the difficulties and costs of entering that gate, we must be assured by the promise of Christ that such a path leads to life. At this stage in the Sermon on the Mount, it is quite clear that this good life which Jesus promises does not guarantee ease and comfort, for he clearly reveals that following him could very likely lead to persecution and scorn. However, by his grace, these things now become blessings.

That is the radical beauty of the gospel! God does not offer us a hope whereby we are instantly freed from the possibility of suffering and death, but rather transforms suffering and death into a gateway through which we find the fullness of life. This is powerfully and centrally manifest in his own suffering and death on the cross, which is beautifully transformed into the greatest and only hope for all of creation through his resurrection and ascension.

Christ crucified is the narrow gate, and only through him will we find new life as his resurrected body.

It is critical to note that this is Jesus' first warning at the end of his teaching. After all, the greatest threat to our faith is ourselves. Again we are reminded that we are to look for the plank in our own eye, examining our own heart and the choices borne there. Our impulse is to look outside of ourselves to assign the blame for our failings and compromises, but we must nurture the disciplines of self-examination, mutual confession and hopeful affirmation. Jesus has laid out the right path for us, but we must set foot on it, every moment of every day, entering by the gate of his cross to pursue and participate in his kingdom.

When we consider the life of St. Francis, it is not hard to see the power and impact of his faithfulness to God. Yet I cannot help but wonder if he might have still made such a difference even if had he not chosen such a hard path for himself. If he had continued in the family business, perhaps he would have turned his wealth and power toward noble ends. Consider how many more mendicant missionaries he might have supported if he had chosen to be a godly and generous merchant. However, this would have been a great compromise for Francis, a sin against God's clear direction. While I am not suggesting that such a life is, in and of itself, ungodly, it would have been insofar as it was disobedient to the costly call of Christ.

We often look up to people like Francis of Assisi or other women and men of God whom we admire for their radical obedience, but we excuse ourselves from such a life with the justification that we have not been called to "that kind of ministry." After all, God needs people in every field of life, does he not? While Jesus is not calling all of us to live like Francis or Clare of Assisi, and while not all of us are to live in inner-city contexts such as our West End neighborhood—*we are all called to live the words of Jesus every day.* Though the specifics of what that might look like will change, the universal truth of that shared vocation of all Christians is that it will cost us everything, it will be disruptive, risky and messy, and above all, we will be truly blessed.

MASKED WOLVES, BAD FRUIT AND FALSE DISCIPLES

Unfortunately, though our own choices present the most immediate and dangerous threat, there are those who would also mislead us. Jesus warns,

> Watch out for false prophets. They come to you in sheep's clothing, but inwardly they are ferocious wolves. By their fruit you will recognize them. Do people pick grapes from thornbushes, or figs from thistles? Likewise every good tree bears good fruit, but a bad tree bears bad fruit. A good tree cannot bear bad fruit, and a bad tree cannot bear good fruit. Every tree that does not bear good fruit is cut down and thrown into the fire. Thus, by their fruit you will recognize them. (Matthew 7:15-20)

While some might be intentionally bent on destruction, many of these false prophets will look just like the rest of us. It is all too easy for us to assume these "wolves in sheep's clothing" will be cartoonishly obvious in their villainy, but Jesus warns that we need discernment to see them for what they are. He reminds us again that the quality of their character is a measure of their heart, which in turn will prove itself true or false by the fruit of their actions.

Without minimizing the importance of sound doctrine, this is why it is critical that we don't rely primarily on what people say they believe; we must pay closer attention to how they express their beliefs in their actions. In this sense, Jesus is not so much warning us about those who are distorting the doctrines of the faith (something we must also be very weary of) but rather about the more subtle, common and insidious corruption of a faith di-

vorced from action. Why is it more common? Because most of
know how we *should* live out the teachings of Christ, yet too often
we settle into the status quo of nominal obedience, emphasizing
our articulated beliefs rather than focusing on our living and active faith. When challenged, we often cite our sinful imperfection
and dependence on grace as a way to minimize or dismiss the indictment of our compromises. Whatever the reasons or excuses,
Jesus strongly warns against this.

Jesus is not teaching that our actions make us righteous or
earn us our salvation. Rather, he is demonstrating that the evidence of a heart transformed by the grace of God is a visible life
of active obedience to his teachings. It is the outward evidence of
our inward nature, formed into the image of Christ, restoring in
us the image of God in which we were created and for which we
were always intended. Yes, the ceremony of my wedding to my
wife formed the covenant bond between us, but what truly makes
us married is the life and relationship that is born out of that
event. In the same way, receiving the unmerited gift of grace in
salvation makes us God's children, but that relationship is proven
true by the loving devotion that is reflected in how we live every
single day.

But what is this fruit? What are we to look for? The Sermon on
the Mount has been describing this fruit from the very beginning,
most vividly in the Beatitudes. Further, in Matthew 12:33-37, we
see that our words also represent the fruit of our hearts. In John
15, Jesus shows that the good fruit that is produced from the vine
of Christ is characterized by sacrificial and selfless love for others.
Later, in Galatians 5, Paul warns against the very real dangers of
the fruit of our sinful nature—each one proven by external acts,
such as rage, selfishness or idolatry. Then he goes on to beautifully describe the fruit of the Spirit—love, joy, peace, patience,
kindness, goodness, faithfulness, gentleness and self-control—
also made manifest in how we live. These fruits will help us dis-

cern the false teachers and prophets among us.

The challenge of discerning a person by their fruit is that the fruit is not always immediately apparent. After all, as children are growing up, we do not immediately and forever exclude them at the first signs of selfishness or immaturity, but rather through loving discipline we help mold them into the ways of righteousness. We must keep this firmly in mind as we nurture the fragile faith of those who are just discovering Christ or are new to his body. (Remember the analogy of the little flowers from chapter eleven?) Jesus is not warning against such people. His warning is not designed to keep the immature believer out of the community but rather to protect the community against those who claim to speak for God—prophets or teachers—but whose hearts are turned against his ways, which is demonstrated by the fruit of their lives (or lack thereof). They bear the external characteristics of godliness, but their hearts and behavior have not been formed by the teaching we have been given by Jesus in the Sermon.

Sadly, I see this demonstrated all too often where Christian leaders use their influence to champion select causes in the name of Christ while minimizing, ignoring or even contradicting other core teachings of Jesus. It is an indictment against the church that the world sees us as a people who are fiercely opposed to homosexuality and abortion at all costs, yet who prove ourselves deeply compromised through silence, minimization or even rejection of Christ's all-encompassing call to peace, generosity, humility and love. To raise the cross of Christ as a banner over our military, economic and sexist campaigns is to defy and defile the heart of the very gospel made manifest in the humble and total sacrifice of Jesus on the cross. Lord have mercy! *Christ have mercy!*

The choice to exclude or cut someone off from the community of faith as a "false prophet" (or for any reason) should be done with much prayer, great discernment and no small amount of grieving. It concerns me greatly how often Christians take public and joyful pride in their ability to weed out all the "heretics" and "false prophets," not only in their communities but in the wider church world and broader culture. (If you don't believe me, try starting a blog on theology and open up the comment section for anyone to weigh in!)

Even Francis and the orders he inspired faced constant and often bitter scrutiny. For every religious order that was approved by Rome, at least a dozen others were rejected as heretical. In many cases they were dangerously (and even violently) heretical, but many simply pushed too hard with legitimate prophetic corrections, earning them excommunication and even death. We need truly prophetic voices for God in the church and in the world, but do not be too quick to fill that role. After all, the "measure you use" to judge others "will be measured to you."

Not stopping there, Jesus goes on to make himself abundantly clear:

> Not everyone who says to me, "Lord, Lord," will enter the kingdom of heaven, but only he who does the will of my Father who is in heaven. Many will say to me on that day, "Lord, Lord, did we not prophesy in your name, and in your name drive out demons and perform many miracles?" Then I will tell them plainly, "I never knew you. Away from me, you evildoers!" (Matthew 7:21-23)

It is not enough to call ourselves Christians. It is not enough to participate in the rituals and practices of status quo religion. Even if, in the name of God, we prophesy or have authority over demons or even perform great miracles, this is no guarantee that God counts us as one of his children. Here Jesus is again reminding us that the righteousness of the Pharisees is not adequate. It would be too easy for us to take these teachings and set up a religious system of external practices that qualify us as "righteous." Yes, we demonstrate our fidelity to him by the way we actively obey his commandments, but it is not these actions themselves that make us faithful; it is rather a submitted and transformed heart that makes them genuine. Simply to believe right doctrine and live moral lives, while deeply important, is not enough. Of course we must confess with our mouths and believe in our hearts that Jesus Christ is Lord, but this does not primarily mean an allegiance to a moral, ethical or religious system; rather, it means active devotion to our very real God.

This is why Jesus stresses that it is the will of our heavenly *Father* that we obey. God, the loving and relational Father, truly *knows us* and longs for us to *know him*. He desires for us real, active and dynamic relationship with him. He is a very present God who will not be satisfied by our most fervent devotion to his ideals or even worship of his majesty as King and Lord if we do not also love him wholly as our Father, which will manifest itself in selfless love of others, that is, love with the same level of interest as we show to ourselves. He calls us to love him in a way that surpasses all these other aspects of submission to him. Here at the end of the Sermon on the Mount, Jesus reminds us again that we are called to love, above all else, for we are called to a God who is the fullness of love himself.

> If I speak in the tongues of men and of angels, but have not love, I am only a resounding gong or a clanging cymbal. If I have the gift of prophecy and can fathom all mysteries and all knowledge, and if I have a faith that can move mountains, but have not love, I am nothing. If I give all I possess to the poor and surrender my body to the flames, but have not love, I gain nothing. (1 Corinthians 13:1-3)

As 1 Corinthians goes on to describe, the true love of our transformed heart is demonstrated in tangible and visible ways. In Luke's Sermon on the Plain, the parallel warning is more clear and specific: "Why do you call me, 'Lord, Lord,' and do not do what I say?" (Luke 6:46).

Jesus' intentions here could not be more clear. Our faithfulness to him is proven by *doing* what he teaches us to do. Stuart Murray points out that one of the most destructive aspects of Christendom Christianity on the church today is how Jesus is worshiped rather than followed. Of the intentional reinterpretations of the Sermon on the Mount which reduced its place as a central teaching for Christian behavior, Murray writes:

> These strategies ensured that the teaching of Jesus could be simultaneously honored and ignored. In the same way, by recasting him as a remote, imperial figure and emphasizing his divinity much more than his humanity, the imperial church could worship and honor Jesus without needing to listen to him, imitate his example, or follow him. Jesus could be effectively marginalized without apparently being dishonored.[2]

This is our heritage as Christians in the Western world. While not absolute, these dynamics have deeply shaped how we read Scripture and apply it in our lives. It is this very tendency that Jesus is warning against in his closing admonitions. God is to be both worshiped and followed. Obedience is better than sacrifice. This is Christ's call to true belief. Jesus said, "I am the way and *the truth* and the life"—he *is* the truth. Truth is made manifest in the incarnation of the living, breathing, moving Jesus. Salvation does not come through the *idea* or even the *message* of his death and resurrection, but in the very real act itself. In the same way, our beliefs are truest when we live them incarnationally, as his resurrected body, united and empowered by his Spirit for the glory of our loving heavenly Father. We are not saved by works, but without those incarnational works our faith is dead.

This devotion must touch every part of our lives, both public and private. No time or place or circumstance is exempt from this radical call to absolute obedience. It is the one path, the one gate, the one and only way. It is Jesus Christ. And that is the message of the entire Sermon on the Mount. It does not describe Christianity or even a high Christian ideal or ethic. Instead, it describes Christ himself.

Conclusion

The Wise Builder (or "Go and Do Likewise")

Matthew 7:24-29

As Little Flowers Community continued to be established as a group of missional Christians sharing life together in our neighborhood, it wasn't long before some were asking the inevitable question: Are we going to get a church building? Our group has always met on the main floor of our community house, which is to say, our living room, dining room and kitchen. In addition to making our shared meal easier, it was essentially the only space we had available, especially with our budget (which was zero). While none of us are opposed to traditional church buildings, we realized that one of the dynamics that drew people to us from our neighborhood was the personal dynamic. It is one thing to come into a neighbor's house for a meal and then choose whether or not to stay for worship, but for many, the idea of entering a traditional church building triggered many of the fears, uncertainties and even wounds that are all too common. We agreed that, in our context, having our meeting place less formal was important.

However, the question began to stir my imagination. If we were to have another building in the community for our life together as a church, what would it look like? Inspired by several stories I had heard through Tom and Christine Sine, I got the idea of getting a building in which we could not only build life together as a faith community, but where people could share everyday life together in intentional community and practice radical hospitality. Given our significant lack of resources, such a dream was just that—a dream. However, I wrote a blog post casting the vision of what I believed this shared-housing community of faith might look like. Several people read the post and strongly resonated with its vision, but it was an e-mail I received from my friend Norm Voth that took me completely by surprise: he thought it was a vision worth pursuing![1]

As director of evangelism and service ministries for Mennonite Church Manitoba, and being the co-conspirator in the formation of Little Flowers, Norm was convinced that if we shared this vision with the right people, they just might get behind us and make it happen. And that is exactly what began to unfold. With the initial promise of backing from a group of Christian businessmen, Norm and I began the hunt for a building in the neighborhood that would suit our needs. What we did not realize was that we were in for a long journey in which we would receive a thorough and often disheartening education on inner-city housing.

A SOLID FOUNDATION

For more than a year we viewed every large building to come on the market in our community. Many were vacant, with the former tenants having been evicted due to a sanitation or fire problem, while others were occupied, and the current tenants welcomed us into their tiny, impoverished rooms with humbling hospitality (though a few were clearly cowed into submission by bullying landlords). A few of the buildings were gutted right to the studs and then left to sit, a common practice for developers with bigger visions than budgets and planning skills, leaving a neighborhood already facing a housing crisis with even fewer places to live.

Wherever we went, no matter the size, age or apparent condition of the building, we always looked at one thing more than any other: the foundation. We were blown away time and again how even the slightest shift in the foundation of a building could wreak havoc on the rest of the structure. Every offer we made on any building was conditional on an engineer's inspection, with the requirement that the structure (namely, the foundation) was sound. One building was in many ways ideal for our needs, both in layout and in location, yet the north corner of the building had sunk into a particularly clay-rich section of the soil, buckling walls, cracking the foundation and twisting much the building's remaining structure. No matter how many aspects of the building were well suited to us, no matter how ideal the size and location were, because that foundation was so questionable, we were forced to pass on it and keep looking.

In this respect, Jesus' closing analogy of the wise and foolish builders paints a pretty clear picture for us and even more so for the people of Israel hearing his words.

> Therefore everyone who hears these words of mine and puts them into practice is like a wise man who built his house on the rock. The rain came down, the streams rose, and the winds blew and beat against that house; yet it did not fall, because it had its foundation on the rock. But everyone who hears these words of mine and does not put them into practice is like a foolish man who built his house on sand. The rain came down, the streams rose, and the winds blew and beat against that house, and it fell with a great crash. (Matthew 7:24-27)

Without the benefit of our modern technology, and given the

heavy clay content of the soil, digging a foundation was brutal and grueling work for the people of Jesus' time, especially under an oven-hot sun. Given the amount of work involved, those listening to Jesus' parable would sympathize with the impulse to cut corners and build without a solid foundation. However, they ultimately would agree with Jesus that such a person would indeed be quite foolish. It should be noted that Matthew's text does not mention this digging, but instead says the wise man built his house on a rock. However, with Luke's parallel reference to digging (Luke 6:46-49) and the reality that, even where stone was present, most builders would have had to dig into the soil to reach it, the principle remains the same: to assure the stability and security of the house, we need a solid foundation. Failing to do so will not only assuredly cost us our home, but potentially kill us and our entire family in the process when the whole thing comes down on our heads.

Like many other Christians, I was raised with this story most commonly being retold in the form of a children's worship song. The basic moral of the little song/parable was to "build your life on the Lord Jesus Christ," meaning ask Jesus to be your Lord and Savior, and be a good Christian. In itself, that is not a bad message to teach children, but as I matured as a Christian and grew into adulthood, that was as far as my understanding of the text went. This casual treatment of the text as a simple parable, pulling it away from the broader context of the whole Sermon on the Mount, robs us of the power and significance of Jesus' words. In such a teaching it was expected that the closing words of a rabbi would be especially significant, and this parable is no exception.

First, it is important to remember Jesus' words at the beginning of this parable. He said in verse 24: "Therefore everyone who hears these words of mine and puts them into practice is like a wise man who built his house on the rock." As we have seen before, Jesus' use of the word *therefore* in this context suggests that his following words are commentary on all that he has said up to this point. He confirms this by stating what his expectations are for his followers: to *hear these words* and to *put them into practice*. Therefore, we see that not only does Jesus link this parable with the whole of his message, but that (again) his expectation is that we *do* what he commands us to do. In other words (and I think it is obvious to any reader), the point of Jesus' entire Sermon on the Mount is to teach us *how to live*. He is not saying we are wise if we become Christians, but rather that we are wise if we respond to the call of discipleship and actively obey the very teachings he has just given us in this text.

This parable is not to be understood as a teaching about the Christian (the wise person) versus the non-Christian (the foolish person). Just like in the previous section of the Sermon where both sides call Jesus "Lord," here both sides work for the same end: to build a house. The foolish person is not someone who rejects Christ, but someone who seeks to claim him as Lord without being faithful in doing so according to Jesus' teachings. As we saw in chapter twelve, it is like the person who chooses the lower diving platform or simply slips into the water from poolside, rationalizing that the end is ultimately the same. It is not the act of "building" that is central (though that is indeed necessary), just as prophesying, casting out demons or performing miracles is not, in itself, the ultimate point. It is not about going to church, being morally upright, or participating in Christian ministry and mission (though they are also all of significant importance). Rather it is only the foundation of full and uncompromising submission to the lordship of Christ, and living out his teaching, that makes us wise builders.

We must remember that in the parable the houses are not proven strong or weak until they are hit by storms. The house built of sand can seem to be firm and solid in times of prosperity and comfort. We too readily believe we have built on a firm foundation when the true testing has not come. Perhaps that is one of the single greatest dangers we face in being Christians in Western contexts, where the relative freedom creates a greater risk of complacency and compromise. This is why Jesus reminds us that where much is given, much is expected. This is why he warned of the difficulty the wealthy and powerful face in entering the kingdom of God. This is why, so often, the persecuted and suffering churches around the world seem to thrive beyond expectation. Those without firm foundations have already been swept away, leaving those who are willing to pay the price of the costly kingdom built on the foundation of living as Christ taught, regardless of circumstances. *Blessed are the poor!*

During my visit to Haiti following the earthquake that devastated the nation, talk of "firm foundations"—both literal and spiritual—were powerfully poignant. The Christians I met in Haiti proved the truth of Jesus' words, that faith is tested in the storms that come upon us in our lives. In his heartbreakingly honest exploration of these questions, Kent Annan reminds us:

> Faith can seem certain. A sense of peace or clarity, the mysterious beauty of life, or the transformations seen in yourself, in someone else, in a community—it couldn't be other than God. But there are also shocks to the system when God seems either absent or negligent. Do we ignore these shocks and their aftershocks? Sometimes a crisis of faith happens in an instant; other times it's a drift into uncertainty. Welcome confirmations of faith. And just as important, pay attention to the crises of doubt or unanswered questions. Honest faith doesn't deny God, but it doesn't deny the uncertain and painful reality of life either.[2]

It is only on the foundation of Jesus that such faith can be born and survive.

THE CORNERSTONE

The implications of Jesus' words go even further. His closing parable would have been a powder keg among his listeners. Those of us who lack the personal or learned understanding of the Jewish messianic expectations often miss the deeper, prophetic implications of this parable. His reference to these two houses being built—one doomed for its lack of foundation, the other solidly established on a firm foundation—would have immediately brought to mind the prophetic words of Isaiah 28:14-18. The parallels between these two texts are hard to ignore, yet I have found that they are rarely commented on in much detail. (For this understanding, I am indebted to Kenneth Bailey's essential volume *Jesus Through Middle Eastern Eyes*.[3])

Isaiah says:

> Therefore hear the word of the LORD, you scoffers
>   who rule this people in Jerusalem.
> You boast, "We have entered into a covenant with death,
>   with the grave we have made an agreement.
> When an overwhelming scourge sweeps by,
>   it cannot touch us,
> for we have made a lie our refuge
>   and falsehood our hiding place." (28:14-15)

Here the prophet is addressing God's people as they are poised to confront an invading Assyrian enemy. Desperate to survive the impending destruction, Israel makes a pact with Egypt to be allies in this coming battle. Isaiah dismisses this pact as nothing more than a "covenant with death." He likens it to building a house on lies and falsehood that will inevitably be overwhelmed and swept away, leaving the people beaten down, unsaved by their empty pact with Egypt. It is clear that Isaiah is calling their faithless covenant with the enemy a weak foundation that will be leveled at the first encounter with the coming storm of Assyrians. This alone would have been enough for the Jews who listened to Jesus to make a connection. However, it is what is at the heart of Isaiah's rebuke that most assuredly proved Christ's intentions with this parable.

In the very center of the text, intentionally situated using a common literary device meant to highlight its importance, the prophet declares:

So this is what the Sovereign LORD says:

"See, I lay a stone in Zion,
    a tested stone,
a precious cornerstone for a sure foundation;
    the one who trusts will never be dismayed.
I will make justice the measuring line
    and righteousness the plumb line." (28:16-17)

In the face of sure destruction because of the false foundation of their compromise, Isaiah makes this declaration of a future hope, the messianic promise of a true cornerstone with a solid foundation. We have the benefit of hindsight to know that Jesus was the fulfillment of the messianic promise, yet for the Jewish people of his day, this was still an eagerly awaited but thus far unrealized hope. However, in declaring that obedience to him is like building on this solid foundation, Jesus is declaring that this awaited hope is realized in him. Not only is he claiming his identity as the promised Messiah, but he is also saying that the messianic hope for God's kingdom is available to all those who obey his teaching. *He* is the cornerstone, the firm foundation! *He* is the long-expected Messiah. In one powerful declaration Jesus shatters any possibility that his teachings are merely a set of worthy ethics or noble ideals. He pins on them the very hope for all creation.

The Sermon on the Mount is not merely the ideals of Christianity or even a core Christian ethic; it is nothing less than Jesus himself. He is the narrow gate and the straight path. He is the only vine that produces good fruit in and through us. He is the sure and only foundation on which our lives and faith have any hope of being firmly built. He is every blessing of the community of the Beatitudes. It is not enough to declare him Lord (though, of course, we must do this). We must demonstrate our submission to his lordship through active obedience to the explicit teachings he has given us here and throughout his life. We are not saved by this obedient devotion to the work he commands, but rather Jesus is saying that if we hear his words, declare him Lord and affirm his teaching, yet do not do what he teaches, then we are fools. "You are my friends if you do what I command. I no longer call you servants, because a servant does not know his master's business. Instead, I have called you friends, for everything that I learned from my Father I have made known to you" (John 15:14-15). True belief in Christ is a devotion born of love that cannot help but seek to do the will of our loving Father—not by our own merit or strength but by the power of the Holy Spirit, who unites us as his people, his body, his church.

It was with this authority that Jesus taught the people. And this authority amazed the crowds and distinguished Jesus from the teachers of the law. They taught with the borrowed authority of the Law and the Prophets. Jesus was and is the fulfillment of the Law and the Prophets, of all righteousness and justice. His authority reached beyond what he said and was demonstrated in how he lived. Indeed, the people were truly amazed, as we should be too. However, Jesus does not ask for our amazement. He asks for our uncompromising and loving obedience, even unto death. Again, he is not only a God who is worthy of all our worship and praise; he is also our Lord and Master, deserving our unwavering obedience. And unlike a bondage of fear to the letter of the law, our obedience is borne out of love, freely and gladly given.

DO LIKEWISE

Little Flowers Community is far from perfect. Those of us who call it our home know all too well the failings, flaws and foibles of our motley crew of misfit Christians. We do not put forth the challenge of this book because, somehow, we have arrived or achieved it. Rather, in our mutual brokenness we daily seek to stand together, and by the power of God's Spirit we are genuinely devoted to trying to hear Jesus' words, see his example and *do likewise*. We are driven by the realization that it is not only important that we are followers of Jesus, but it is also important what that means, how that affects the way we live individually, but more so together as a people. It is as much about *how* we believe as it is about *what* and *why*. And while we have a long way to go in building on the foundation of Christ, we have caught powerful and humbling glimpses of his kingdom, encounters with the transforming grace and love of God in otherwise devastating and hopeless circumstances.

Without question Jesus' teaching in the Sermon on the Mount is demanding. He warned us as much, from beginning to end. Following Jesus is not simply about learning a few important lessons that we apply to our life to make us better people. This is a dangerous teaching to follow. John Stott warns:

> In applying this teaching to ourselves, we need to consider that the Bible is a dangerous book to read, and that the church is a dangerous society to join. For in reading the Bible we hear the words of Christ, and in joining the church we say we believe in Christ. As a result, we belong to the company described by Jesus as both hearing his teaching and calling him Lord. Our membership therefore lays upon us a serious responsibility of ensuring that what we know and what we say is translated into what we do.[4]

Stott is pointing to far more than what we have come to know as *application*. Instead, he is calling us to consider the very real and demanding *implications* of Jesus' words and example. In application, we take a new insight, idea or truth and apply it to our existing way of life, like adding a LEGO block on top of another. Considering the implications requires that we examine our entire way of life—our assumptions, our expectations and our every choice—in light of this new understanding or conviction. It is being willing to make any change, no matter how difficult or demanding, if it means being more faithful as a disciple of Jesus Christ. For many of us at Little Flowers, the implications of Jesus' teaching in the Sermon on the Mount have been very real. It means changing where we live, how we spend our money and the way we understand personal ownership. We did not formulate a firm set of rules or standards, but rather carefully, humbly and intentionally began to make choices that we believed were essential to living faithfully. It has been difficult and demanding, but it has been stunningly worth it.

It is our hope that this book, with its stories and reflections from our small corner of the world, will help encourage and inspire you and your community to consider the implications of the Sermon on the Mount for your lives. Genuinely take the time to "hear" the words of Jesus in this powerful teaching, then go and do likewise! Doing so means willingly choosing to live in the tension between ordinary life and extraordinary belief.

Even before his conversion St. Francis of Assisi was a passionate and gifted poet and songwriter. When he gave his life wholly to the worship and service of Jesus Christ, that did not end but was transformed into something even more beautiful. Some of the earliest poems found in the Italian dialect are songs of praise to God written by Francis. So filled with the joy of the Spirit, he was even known to pick up sticks from the ground and mimic playing the violin, dancing around and worshiping his Savior. Even on his deathbed, Francis took such deep joy in the hope of his salvation that he praised God for "Sister Death," saying:

Happy those she finds doing your most holy will.
The second death can do no harm to them.

Praise and bless my Lord, and give thanks,
and serve him with great humility.[5]

St. Francis of Assisi can appear to be an especially and unreachably holy man whose life and example far surpass our own capacity. Yet the truth is that he was a simple person, just like you and me, who was convinced that Jesus actually means what he says when he invites us, "Come, follow me."

Inspired by Francis's love for well-crafted and prayerful songs to his Creator, the following is a prayer that our humble community prays, inspired by the Sermon on the Mount, but even more so by the Son of Man, the Son of God who lived and embodied it for our sake and the glory of God.

The Little Flowers Community Prayer of Jesus

Lord and Creator, let us embrace the costly blessings which
   you desire for us,
blessings that confound the wisdom and strength of this
   world.
Teach us to be your agents of preservation in a world
   touched by death,
and beacons of hope in a world shrouded in darkness.
Transform us into your image through the crucible of the
   cross,
writing your mandates upon our hearts, made pure by your
   perfect love.
Embolden us to be your ambassadors, living as
   representatives of your holy kingdom,
stirring in us your love for others, especially for those who
   would seek to destroy us because of you.
Make us decrease so that you might increase, as a watching
   world sees you, not us.

Daily we declare that your priorities are ours, even before
    our own needs and desires.
Every moment we live, we live for your glory—the glory of
    a loving Father and a just King.
Free us of any distraction, craving or anxiety that would
    keep us from fully following you.
For we acknowledge that everything we could possibly
    need is yours to give us.
Remind us of our sinful brokenness and your gift of grace
    as we encounter brokenness in others.
You are the answer to our every question. You are the
    treasure that we desperately seek,
and it is you who invites us into your salvation, as prodigals
    returning to the Father's embrace.
Keep us upon your path of righteousness and justice,
    bearing the good fruit of your Spirit,
for it is on you, Lord Jesus, that all hope is built, for all of
    creation, now and forever more.
Amen.

Notes

Introduction

[1]When you include all Franciscans—First, Second and Third Orders throughout the various Christian traditions—and all that has been written about him and the movement he birthed, Francis is arguably the most influential Christian figure outside of the biblical record.

[2]While Jesus might not have given this exact message as it is recorded, when taken in light of his later teachings and example, the other Gospel records, and the practices of the early church, it is fair to assume that this Gospel's author is representing an intentional, organized collection of teachings that accurately reflect the core of Jesus' message.

[3]In a pleasant coincidence, both Francis and I come from an Italian father and a French mother.

[4]We are affiliated with the Mennonite Church Manitoba.

[5]Francis never intended to start a religious order; rather, he was seeking to form a life of faithfulness to Christ for all people. This later inspired him to offer an adapted way of life for those who were not called to the absolute vows of poverty or celibacy.

[6]Dietrich Bonhoeffer, *The Cost of Discipleship* (New York: Touchstone, 1995), p. 89.

[7]Scot McKnight, *One.Life: Jesus Calls, We Follow* (Grand Rapids: Zondervan, 2010), p. 31.

Chapter 1: Setting the Stage

[1]Stanley Hauerwas, *Matthew,* Brazos Theological Commentary on the Bible (Grand Rapids: Brazos, 2006), p. 51.

[2]In the years since we moved here, all of those drug houses have since been closed and replaced with many wonderful neighbors.

[3]Hauerwas, *Matthew,* p. 59.

Chapter 2: Blessed Are the Poor in Spirit

[1]Kenneth E. Bailey, *Jesus Through Middle Eastern Eyes* (Downers Grove, Ill.: IVP Academic, 2008), p. 68, italic in original.

[2]Like the Jews of Jesus' time, it is too easy for those of us reading the Gospels today to dismiss the Pharisees and Sadducees as puritanical extremists. However, an honest look at Scripture and at our place as Christians in the world today strongly suggests that we read ourselves into these narratives in the place of these very men.

[3]John Stott, *Christian Counter-Culture: The Message of the Sermon on the Mount* (Downers Grove, Ill.: InterVarsity Press, 1978), p. 38.

[4]Ibid., p. 39.

[5]Kenneth Baxter Wolf, *The Poverty of Riches* (New York: Oxford University Press, 2003).

[6]On new monasticism see "New Monasticism," *Wikipedia*, http://en.wiki pedia.org/wiki/New_Monasticism. On the "abandoned places of the Empire" see "Who Are/What the New Monasticism Is," New Monasticism, www.thesimpleway.org/about/12-marks-of-new-monasticism/.

[7]Most people involved in new monasticism are aware of these dynamics and are intentionally seeking to address them. I am speaking here more to the popular movement of people and communities that are often well-intentioned but less aware and intentional about these realities.

[8]For an excellent exploration of these issues, see David Fitch, "Why the Missional/Emerging Church Is So Young and White," Reclaiming the Mission, January 16, 2009, www.reclaimingthemission.com/why-the-missional emerging-church-is-so-young-and-white.

[9]Stott, *Christian Counter-Culture*, p. 40.

[10]Kent Annan, *Following Jesus Through the Eye of the Needle: Living Fully, Loving Dangerously* (Downers Grove, Ill.: InterVarsity Press, 2009).

Chapter 3: Blessed Are the Mourners and the Meek

[1]In fact, the expression "inherit the land" also occurs in Psalm 37:9, 29, both describing who would "inherit the land." In these cases it was to be inherited by "those who hope in the LORD" and "the righteous" (NIV 2011). These other qualifications help inform our understanding of meekness.

[2]These events are often cited as the reason for the Franciscans having been the custodians of the Holy Land for Christianity for so long.

Chapter 4: Blessed Are the Justice Cravers, the Merciful and the Pure in Heart

[1]John Driver, *Kingdom Citizens* (Scottdale, Penn.: Herald Press, 1980), p. 65.

[2]For a brilliant unpacking of the centrality of this text, see Scot McKnight, *The Jesus Creed* (Brewster, Mass.: Paraclete, 2004).

[3]I highly recommend Adam Taylor, *Mobilizing Hope: Faith-Inspired Activism for a Post–Civil Rights Generation* (Downers Grove, Ill.: InterVarsity Press, 2010).

[4]Some historians speculate that Francis's later experience with stigmata— bearing on his own body the wounds of the crucified Christ—was in fact the open lesions of leprosy that he had contracted in his years of close service among the afflicted. If this is true, it still beautifully illustrates how Francis, out of love, bore the suffering of others on his own body, even unto death.

[5]*Entertaining Angels*, directed by Michael Ray Rhodes (Pacific Palisades, Calif.: Paulist Pictures, 1996), VHS, 110 min.

Chapter 5: Blessed Are the Peacemakers and the Persecuted

[1]John Driver, *Kingdom Citizens* (Scottdale, Penn.: Herald Press, 1980), p. 68.

[2]The concept of the "myth of redemptive violence" is presented by Walter Wink in *The Powers That Be,* Galilee Trade paperback ed. (New York: Doubleday, 1999).

Chapter 6: Of Salt, Light and the Law

[1]Dewi Hughes, *Power and Poverty* (Downers Grove, Ill.: IVP Academic, 2008), p. 138.

[2]Stanley Hauerwas, *Matthew,* Brazos Theological Commentary on the Bible (Grand Rapids: Brazos, 2006), p. 68.

[3]Martin Luther King Jr., *Strength to Love,* deluxe ed. (Minneapolis: Fortress, 2010), p. 29-30.

Chapter 7: Oaths, Eyes and Enemies

[1]Borrowing from Shakespeare, *Hamlet,* act 3, scene 2, lines 222-23.

[2]Dietrich Bonhoeffer, *The Cost of Discipleship* (New York: Touchstone, 1995), p. 140.

[3]Ibid., p. 143.

Chapter 8: Hiding in Plain Sight

[1]As I sat down to write this chapter, I immediately ran into a problem: How do I illustrate what it means to *not* perform our obedience in order to be seen by others without doing just that? In the end I decided that I would tell stories of others in my community, people who would be very unlikely to blow their own horn and therefore illustrate well the very thing I am talking about here.

[2]An essential and practical resource for churches and Christian ministries on this topic is Brian Fikkert and Steve Corbett's *When Helping Hurts: How to Alleviate Poverty Without Hurting the Poor . . . and Yourself* (Chicago: Moody Publishers, 2009).

[3]Dietrich Bonhoeffer, *The Cost of Discipleship* (New York: Touchstone, 1995), pp. 164-65.

[4]I personally have found the prayer breviary produced by the Missio Dei community to be particularly helpful. See http://hermitjrnl.files.wordpress.com/2010/01/missio_dei_breviary_2.pdf.

[5]John Michael Talbot, *The Lessons of St. Francis* (New York: Plume, 1998), p. 226.

[6]Scot McKnight, *Fasting*, The Ancient Practices (Nashville: Thomas Nelson, 2009), p. xxi.

[7]For an excellent and challenging exploration of this ancient spiritual discipline, I highly commend to you Scot McKnight's *Fasting*, a thorough and accessible book on the topic (see ibid.).

Chapter 9: The Disciple's Prayer

[1]See Kenneth E. Bailey's *Jesus Through Middle Eastern Eyes* (Downers Grove, Ill.: IVP Academic, 2008) for an excellent exploration of this subject in respect to Jewish culture and the Lord's Prayer.

[2]See ibid., pp. 119-23.

[3]"Quando dou comida aos pobres chamam-me de santo. Quando pergunto por que eles são pobres chamam-me de communista." Quoted in Zildo Rocha, *Helder, o Dom: uma vida que marcou os rumos da Igreja no Brasil* (Petrópolis, Brazil: Editora Vozes, 2000), p. 53.

[4]Bailey, *Jesus Through Middle Eastern Eyes*, p. 126.

Chapter 10: A Confident Kingdom

[1]Stanley Hauerwas, *Matthew*, Brazos Theological Commentary on the Bible (Grand Rapids: Brazos, 2006), pp. 80-81.

[2]Ibid., p. 81.

Chapter 11: From Judgment to Humility

[1]Stanley Hauerwas, *Matthew*, Brazos Theological Commentary on the Bible (Grand Rapids: Brazos, 2006), p. 85.

[2]It should be noted here that walking away is our last resort. While we mustn't attempt to push our faith on those unwilling to receive it, neither should this Scripture justify writing people off because they are simply too difficult for us. Love is tenacious and long-suffering.

[3]Dewi Hughes, *Power and Poverty* (Downers Grove, Ill.: IVP Academic, 2008), p. 149.

[4]John Michael Talbot, *The Lessons of St. Francis* (New York: Plume, 1998), p. 133.

Chapter 12: Gates and Fruit

[1]Dietrich Bonhoeffer, *The Cost of Discipleship* (New York: Touchstone, 1995), p. 58.

[2]Stuart Murray, *The Naked Anabaptist* (Scottdale, Penn.: Herald Press, 2010), p. 54.

Conclusion

[1]Since writing this, we have found and purchased a building where we have begun development of a new missional-monastic community called Chiara House (*Chiara* being the Italian name for Clare of Assisi). See http://chiara house.ca for more details.

[2]Kent Annan, *After Shock* (Downers Grove, Ill.: IVP Books, 2011), p. 17.

[3]Kenneth E. Bailey, *Jesus Through Middle Eastern Eyes* (Downers Grove, Ill.: IVP Academic, 2008).

[4]John Stott, *The Message of the Sermon on the Mount,* The Bible Speaks Today (Downers Grove, Ill.: InterVarsity Press, 1978), p. 210.

[5]"Canticle of the Sun," *Wikipedia,* http://en.wikipedia.org/wiki/Canticle_of_ the_Sun.

Recommended Reading

While by no means an exhaustive list of the books I benefited from in writing this book, the following titles represent a strong core of what influenced my thinking.

SERMON ON THE MOUNT

Bailey, Kenneth E. *Jesus Through Middle Eastern Eyes: Cultural Studies in the Gospels*. Downers Grove, Ill.: IVP Academic, 2008.

Bonhoeffer, Dietrich. *The Cost of Discipleship*. New York: Touchstone, 1995.

Driver, John. *Kingdom Citizens*. Scottdale, Penn.: Herald Press, 1980.

Greenman, Jeffrey P., Timothy Larsen and Stephen R. Spencer, eds. *The Sermon on the Mount Through the Centuries: From the Early Church to John Paul II*. Grand Rapids: Brazos, 2007.

Hauerwas, Stanley. *Matthew*. Brazos Theological Commentary on the Bible. Grand Rapids: Brazos, 2006.

Hughes, Dewi. *Power and Poverty: Divine and Human Rule in a World of Need*. Downers Grove, Ill.: IVP Academic, 2008.

Jordan, Clarence. *Sermon on the Mount*. Valley Forge, Penn.: Judson Press, 1952.

Miller, John W. *The Christian Way: A Guide to the Christian Life based on the Sermon on the Mount*. Scottdale, Penn.: Herald Press, 1976.

Murray, Stuart. *The Naked Anabaptist*. Scottdale, Penn.: Herald Press, 2010.

Stassen, Glen H. *Living the Sermon on the Mount: A Practical Hope for Grace and Deliverance*. San Francisco: Jossey-Bass, 2006.

Stott, John R. W. *The Message of the Sermon on the Mount*. The Bible Speaks Today. Downers Grove, Ill.: InterVarsity Press, 1978.

THE BEATITUDES

Bessenecker, Scott A. *How to Inherit the Earth: Submitting Ourselves to a Servant Savior*. Downers Grove, Ill.: InterVarsity Press, 2009.

Cantalamess, Raniero. *Beatitudes: Eight Steps to Happiness*. Cincinnati, Ohio: Servant Books, 2009.

Forest, Jim. *The Ladder of the Beatitudes*. Maryknoll, N.Y.: Orbis, 1999.

Sheen, Fulton J. *The Cross and the Beatitudes: Lessons on Love and Forgiveness*. Liguori, Mo.: Liguori/Triumph, 2000.

Trzyna, Thomas. *Blessed Are the Pacifists: The Beatitudes and Just War Theory*. Scottdale, Penn.: Herald Press, 2006.

THE LORD'S PRAYER

Haase, Albert. *Living the Lord's Prayer: The Way of the Disciple*. Downers Grove, Ill.: InterVarsity Press, 2009.

Mulholland, James. *Praying Like Jesus: The Lord's Prayer in a Culture of Prosperity*. New York: HarperCollins, 2001.

Wright, N. T. *The Lord and His Prayer*. Grand Rapids: Eerdmans, 1996.

ST. FRANCIS AND THE FRANCISCANS

Bessenecker, Scott A. *The New Friars: The Emerging Movement Serving the World's Poor*. Downers Grove, Ill.: InterVarsity Press, 2006.

Boff, Leonardo. *Francis of Assisi: A Model for Human Liberation*. Maryknoll, N.Y.: Orbis, 2006.

Bonaventure. *The Life of St. Francis*. San Francisco: HarperSan-Francisco, 2005.

Chesterton, G. K. *Saint Francis of Assisi*. New York: Image Books, 1990.

Cron, Ian Morgan. *Chasing Francis: A Pilgrim's Tale*. Colorado Springs: NavPress, 2006.

Cunningham, Lawrence S. *Francis of Assisi: Performing the Gospel Life*. Grand Rapids: Eerdmans, 2004.

Hopcke, Robert H., and Paul A. Schwartz. *Little Flowers of Francis of Assisi: A New Translation*. Boston: New Seeds, 2006.

Kauffman, Ivan J. *Follow Me: A History of Christian Intentionality*. Eugene, Ore.: Cascade Books, 2009.

Short, William J. *Poverty and Joy: The Franciscan Tradition*. London: Darton, Longman & Todd, 2005.

Spoto, Donald. *Reluctant Saint: The Life of Francis of Assisi*. New York: Penguin Compass, 2002.

Talbot, John Michael. *The Lessons of St. Francis*. New York: Plume, 1998.

Acknowledgments

I would maintain that thanks are
the highest form of thought,
and that gratitude is happiness
doubled by wonder.

G. K. CHESTERTON

Ultimately, no book is the product of a single person, and that is very true with this book. There is no way I can adequately thank all the people who have made it possible. I am especially thankful to my wife, Kim, whose love, support, encouragement and persistence keep me going every day. I am also grateful to have behind me an amazing family, both in North America and Australia. To all my family, thank you!

The foundation of our ministry has always been those amazing and crazy people we live and serve alongside. Brenden Knight, Michelle Funderburg, Lindsey Ainsworth and Kathryn Hodge—you are the unsung heroes who do so much for so little. You are champions! To Little Flowers Community, the true coauthors of this book, thank you for your love, your challenges and your lovable eccentricities.

Without the perseverance, friendship and vision of my co-conspirator, Norm Voth, none of this would be possible. To Norm and the whole Mennonite Church Manitoba family, thank you!

And last, but far from least, I am eternally grateful to the InterVarsity Press family, who believed in me and this book enough to make it happen. To my editor and fellow traveler, David Zimmerman, you've made this a far better book than I could have done alone, extending friendship to boot! To Adrianna Wright, who saw the potential for this book before I did and persistently encouraged me to write it, thank you. And to all the other Likewise Books authors who helped me through the process, you saved my sanity!

Thank you Almighty God who, by the example of blessed St. Francis, moves us to live the words of Jesus together and gives us hope for his kingdom, now and forever. Amen.

Discussion Guide

At the heart of Jesus' teaching is his call for us to die to self and share in the resurrection into his body, which is the church— the community of faith. The Sermon on the Mount is likewise not meant to be practiced in isolation but rather presumes our relationship with one another as essential to our relationship to God. Jesus' teaching here must therefore be read first and foremost in the context of community. When St. Francis began to follow the teachings of Jesus so radically, community was born. Men and women from all walks of life were drawn to Christ in him and his growing community.

The Cost of Community is also best understood by reading and engaging it with a trusted group of people. How that will look will depend greatly on the context you find yourself in, but community should remain a constant. The following questions divide the Sermon on the Mount into smaller sections, allowing you to reflect on, discuss and experiment with Jesus' teaching. Each section has questions concerning how we think and understand the text (head), questions about our emotions and motivations (heart), and questions about what it looks like to truly live out the teachings of Jesus (hands). My hope is that these questions will just be a start—a launching point into greater depth, passion and practice in your community's pursuit of *living the kingdom together.*

PART 1: **The Community of the Beatitudes (Matthew 5:1-12)**

• HEAD

Before reading *The Cost of Community*, what did you think the Beatitudes meant? How did the blessings relate to you?

In the book we see that the Beatitudes are not an offer of blessings in exchange for certain behaviors but rather represent the present reality of being blessed, even in the midst of our circumstance. How does this distinction change how you understand and engage with the Beatitudes?

• HEART

Think about a time when you were deeply grieved by sin in your life. What response did it produce in you?

How can we foster genuine contrition that will lead to active repentance?

• HANDS

John Driver is quoted as defining *shalom* as

> well-being, or health, or salvation in its fullest sense, material as well as spiritual. It described the situation of well-being which resulted from authentically whole (healed) relationships among people, as well as between persons and God.

Jesus calls us to be peacemakers—makers of shalom—participating as God's children in what he is doing in the world. Consider proactive ways you can start bringing shalom to your neighborhood. Where is the Father at work that you can join him in making shalom?

PART 2: **From the Heart (Matthew 5:13-48)**

• **HEAD**

Christians often have the reputation of being judgmental, able to point out to the world all that is wrong with it. However, when Jesus calls us to be salt and light, his emphasis shifts back to us. It is when we live as the community of the Beatitudes—humble, repentant, meek, hungry for justice, merciful, pure of heart, makers of peace and sufferers with Christ—that we are salt and light. What does this shift of emphasis mean with respect to how we relate to the world and its problems?

• **HEART**

Jesus set the bar high when he said, "I tell you, do not resist an evil person. If anyone slaps you on the right cheek, turn to them the other cheek also." As a concept, we might affirm his "turn the other cheek" policy. However, when we are confronted by the actual circumstances, it is far more difficult. What makes "turning the other cheek" so difficult for us?

What is your natural impulse in such situations? Why?

How can you nurture in your heart the response Jesus requires of us?

• **HANDS**

Jesus calls us to love and pray for our enemies—not those we call enemy, as there should be none of those, but rather those who consider us as such. Who are your "enemies"? Consider how you can actively and concretely love them in ways that are humble and respectful, yet genuine and costly. Make time on a daily basis to pray for them as well.

PART 3: Living the Kingdom (Matthew 6)

• HEAD

Fasting has been a central practice of both Jewish and Christian traditions for centuries. In the Sermon on the Mount, Jesus listed it alongside prayer and giving to those in need. Why do you think fasting is so centrally important to Jesus' teaching on living the kingdom life?

How does Jesus' teaching on the topic challenge your understanding of fasting in your life?

• HEART

Jesus is clearly concerned that when we give to the poor, pray and fast, we do so for the right reasons. This tells us two things:

- that he expects those disciplines to be part of our lives
- that we are examining our intentions—why and how we do them

Spend some time prayerfully considering both points in your own life. Are you consistently practicing these disciplines? If not, why not?

Reflect on how and why you practice these disciplines. Is there any intention that is false? Are there ways in which you could do them more appropriately? Spend time discussing these as well.

• HANDS

The Disciple's Prayer (or the Lord's Prayer) is a beautiful summation of the entire Sermon on the Mount. Commit for two weeks to pray the prayer twice a day—in the morning and evening. You can pray it as it appears directly in Scripture or use the version we created at Little Flowers:

> Father God, who unites us together as one body,
> one family, sister and brother.
> May your name be made holy by your Word
> and by the witness of us, your people.

> May your kingdom be established here and now, in and
>   through us.
> May your will be our first and most immediate priority,
> just as it is to the angels above.
> Provide for us all and only what we need
> for life together and obedience to you.
> Let the gift of your undeserved grace for us overflow
> from us onto those who have wronged us,
> where everything that is owed is fully forgiven.
> Lead us on your path, away from the empty promises
> of our selfish temptations.
> Rescue us from every scheme of sin and darkness
> which would take us from that path.
> For you are King, this is your kingdom and we are your
>   citizens and servants.
> All we are, all we have and all we will do
> is by your power and for your glory alone,
> in the past, in the present and in the future.
> Amen

Or write your own version, especially with others in your community. Or do a combination of options. Whichever way you choose, commit to saying the prayer out loud twice a day for two weeks. Be sure to do so slowly, considering each line as it reflects against your own life, faith community and neighborhood.

PART 4: Building to Last (Matthew 7)

• HEAD

On Jesus' warning that we should not judge one another, Stanley Hauerwas said,

> We are able to see ourselves only through the vision made
> possible by Jesus—a vision made possible by our participa-

tion in a community of forgiveness that allows us to name our sins.

How does this change your understanding about judgment?

How does our commitment to mutual accountability and confession help us overcome our tendency to judge others?

Spend some time as a group brainstorming about healthy way to acknowledge your sin to one another. Be discreet, respectful and gracious, but be honest. What might it look like to intentionally become a community of forgiveness?

• HEART

Few things make us more hesitant to step out and follow Jesus in radical obedience than our fears—fear of what it will cost us, fear of how people will treat us, fear of failing. Yet, in the face of these fears—even in the face of the seemingly impossible circumstances we face—Jesus promises us that he will give us all that we need to fully obey him. All we have to do is ask, seek and knock; in other words, we must be willing to pursue him. Which fears hold you back from stepping out in greater obedience? Share these fears with support friends and ask God to provide what you need to overcome them.

• HANDS

At the end of *The Cost of Community*, I shared the Little Flowers Community Prayer of Jesus, a summation of the entire Sermon on the Mount that we pray together regularly. Consider ways you can creatively and consistently put the Sermon on the Mount in the forefront of your life on a daily basis. Be it a prayer, a song or a commitment to read the entire text of Matthew 5–7 daily, find a way to remind yourself to truly live the teachings of Jesus.

LIKEWISE. *Go and do.*

A man comes across an ancient enemy, beaten and left for dead. He lifts the wounded man onto the back of a donkey and takes him to an inn to tend to the man's recovery. Jesus tells this story and instructs those who are listening to "go and do likewise."

Likewise books explore a compassionate, active faith lived out in real time. When we're skeptical about the status quo, Likewise books challenge us to create culture responsibly. When we're confused about who we are and what we're supposed to be doing, Likewise books help us listen for God's voice. When we're discouraged by the troubled world we've inherited, Likewise books encourage us to hold onto hope.

In this life we will face challenges that demand our response. Likewise books face those challenges with us so we can act on faith.

likewisebooks.com